"Most Americans come home from Ireland with a tweedy cap, a shawl or shillelagh, tales of kissing the Blarney Stone and pub crawls in Dublin; or talk of the priest in the Burren whose earlobes or bald head put ye in mind of your late Uncle Jimmy. Leslie Lee embarks with a scholar's curiosity about attachments and connections, origins and destinations and returns with a deeper understanding of herself, her sisters, her far flung, extended family and the species at large, of the way history and anthropology, geography and genealogy, fantasy, and myth comingle to bring the larger human narrative to bear on we Irish and Americans, we humans, one and all, each and every. Well worth the journey, well worth the read!"

      —Thomas Lynch

D1270664

OTHER BOOKS BY LESLIE LEE

*Backcountry Ranger
in Glacier National Park,
1910-1913:
The Diaries and Photographs
of Norton Pearl*

Published 1994

Sacred Space: Pine Hollow

Published 2014

BOOK **1** LESLIE'S TRAVEL COMPANION

We Are the Land

Ireland

LESLIE LEE

LESLIE LEE PUBLISHER

TRAVERSE CITY, MICHIGAN

Published by
Leslie Lee Publisher
Traverse City, Michigan

Publisher's Cataloging-in-Publication Data
Lee, Leslie.

We are the land : Ireland / Leslie Lee. – Traverse City, MI : Leslie Lee Publisher, 2019.

p. ; cm.

ISBN13: 978-0-9915022-4-0

1. Ireland--History--Pictorial works. 2. Ireland--Description and travel--Pictorial works. 3. Anthropology--Ireland. 4. Ireland--Genealogy. 5. DNA. 6. Heredity--Ireland. I. Title.

DA910.L44 2019
941.5--dc23   2019900580

Illustrations by Leslie Lee
Photography by Elizabeth Evans, Jennifer Hebert, Josephine Ellison

Interior design and layout by Gail Dennis and Leslie Lee
Edited by Jennifer Carroll and Leslie Lee

First edition: March 2019

Printed in the United States of America
23 22 21 20 19 • 5 4 3 2 1

For Josie, Jenni, and Liz

We are the three that is one and the one is the land. We are the
spirit of the place, the essence of the earth and the water, the
forests, the lakes, the cliffs, and the bogs. We are the land.

Banba, Fódla, Ériu
Three Irish Goddesses

PROVINCES
OF IRELAND

Contents

All charts, maps, and illustrations were created by Leslie Lee. Her maps of Ireland are based on an original antique map by Johann Baptist Homann, 1712.

LIST OF ILLUSTRATIONS

List of Maps and Charts

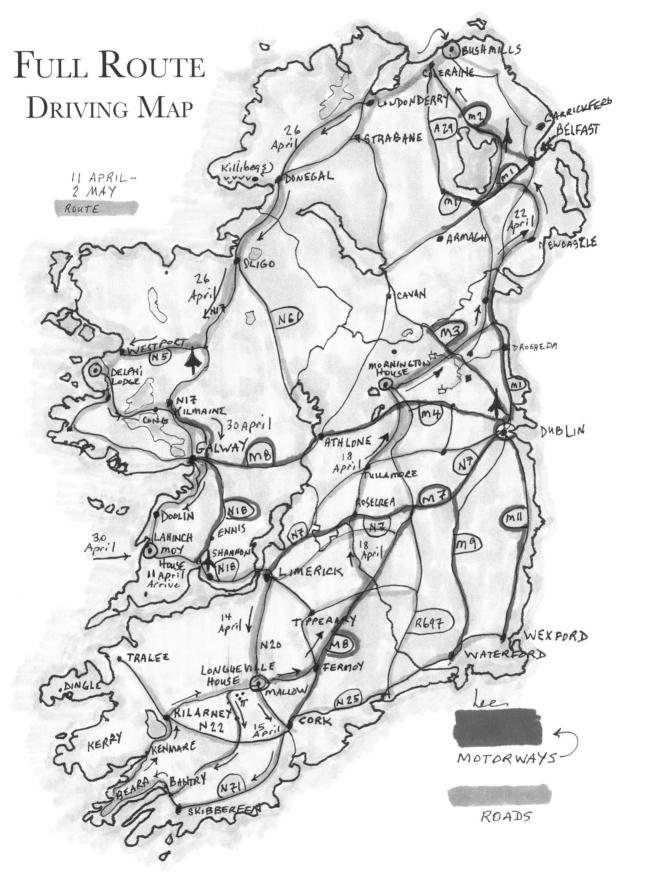

PREFACE

In Search of Who We Are

I'm not a geneticist, a historian, a teacher, or a dendrochronologist. I wasn't born or raised in Ireland though my direct maternal ancestry is Irish. However, I am a student of many and varied subjects. I'm intensely interested in the deep history of my people. This is a story about four sisters returning to their home-land in search of their ancestors, of their introduction to the land and people of Ireland, and of finding each other.

Before we left on our trip, I studied so I would better appreciate my short time there and so we would have pertinent information at our fingertips. I wrote and drew the maps and charts for a pocket size spiral bound hand-written study guide for each of us. It embodied our itineraries, handy data, maps, and charts that we could carry everywhere. Map and chart making takes longer than one might think since a good deal of research goes into their development. But that's what I enjoy. The art accompanying the journal entries in this book was drawn and painted on site, often in the few minutes available before I clambered back behind the wheel of the van. I painted the maps and charts later.

At the last minute before *We Are the Land* was to be published, my editor and I decided to add stanzas of poetry I wrote for my 2014 book titled, *Sacred Space: Pine Hollow.* They seem to work perfectly together as each describes a deep sense of connection and lineage to the land and devotion to the natural world.

I wrote the text for *We Are the Land* at night or in the mornings over coffee, adding to the story when I recalled events back home. Details paint a broad picture for me. Not having the benefit of narrow scholarship in a single field means I'm open to the connections between them, and the criticism of experts as well. Often I've wished to take up a study in depth but there simply isn't enough time in one life. I'd miss the excitement of broad understanding, significance, and insight between genres.

The study guides proved to be so useful on our trip I've incorporated updated versions in this book. I plan to produce a separate pocket version of the study guide because we took them everywhere and wanted to have one on hand during the trip.

Whatever small amount I've learned vastly improved my experience in Ireland. I'm still learning. Let me apologize for any mistakes, they're all mine. I've done my best to include correct dates for prehistoric events. Rather than use the words "approximately, about, sort of, some of," I've taken the liberty to simply state the date I thought was best. I welcome referenced corrections through my website LeeStudioTC.com.

As a person I'm a point on a long line. In Ireland my point found its place in the continuum of deep time. Side by side, my sisters and I shared ourselves with each other in experiences that shaped us into the future. To be on Irish soil felt like finding our mother, the mother of all life, Earth. We journeyed into the past, into the future, and found each other. To all the Irish I've met on my visits who are the land, who have opened their doors, their hearts, and shared their spirit, "Go raibh maith agut." Thank you.

INTRODUCTION

The Journey Home Begins

An ancient soul united with this sacred place
beneath the stars, inside the wind, within the lake.
The voices of my childhood songs and stories form
the fundamental chord of this bequeathed refrain
with harmonies to echo on a thousand years.

~Leslie Lee, *Sacred Space: Pine Hollow, 2014*

Snow scattershot against the windows. I looked up. Alone. I listened to flames futter between pieces of wood and a rising surf thud along the distant shore. How did I get here? How will I find my way home? I raised my children here, but this was not the home of my people. I rested my head back and dreamed of Ireland.

It was the first time in twenty-two years I was without children at home. For sixteen of them, I lived in this turn-of-the-century cottage in a small village on the Lake Michigan shore. I wanted to feel the freedom to leave. Plans of a glorious trip hatched in my mind. First I would host a week with friends, then a week with my two sisters, Liz and Jenni, and our cousin Josie. The trip would be my treat to them and a gift of shared memories to myself. Why Ireland? I'd been to England and Scotland, the land of my ancestors, on earlier trips with my children. Yet family lore was we were English, Scots, and Scotch-Irish.

Were we native Irish as well? I was unsure if we would find the lovely Irish family of our dreams, or if we would find that our family were horse thieves. Would we sisters get along with each other?

Josie's mother was Aunt Mommy to me. She was my mother's identical twin, making us biologically half-sisters. More telling, we were the youngest cousins of eleven who summered together all of our lives on our family's northern Michigan homestead. Eating the dust of nine bigger kids has a way of bonding the youngest two. Later as a young mother, the winter I hurt my back in Chicago, Josie helped with my children while her husband was in cooking school in New York. Since, she and I traveled thousands of miles together with the kids. Josie's a terrific navigator, and I'm a good enough driver, having started driving on the left side of the road when I was younger in the United Kingdom and the Caribbean. Still, the roads of Ireland proved to be difficult, narrow, twisting, and bordered by intruding rock walls of variable sizes and shapes, or harrowing cliffs.

Josie, Jenni, Liz, Leslie

Perhaps it's odd to travel so far in order to get closer. This trip was a first with my two sisters as a way to share good times. In the past we shared some not-so-good ones. Our religious upbringing dominated my childhood until they each went off to college before me. They were believers and I was not.

I left home precipitously at age seventeen, an unbeliever, desperate to get away. This gulf separated us for twenty years despite raising our children during the summers at the same family group of cottages. Over time their religious beliefs evolved to become their own. Even though the healing balm of time helped, unresolved conflicts and mistrust still underlay my relationships with them. This trip seemed risky given the uncertainties and confinement inherent in travel. Still I hoped our shared discoveries and minor adventures would bond us in shared positive memories for the future.

I asked Liz after our journey how she felt when I asked if she wanted to go to Ireland with us.

"I thought it'd be the trip of a lifetime," she said. "I couldn't wait to check out the libraries and historical centers for primary sources and to touch my feet to Irish soil."

I thought to myself then about her love of collecting people, and knew the trip also meant meeting people, our people, new people, and perhaps, important people. As a teacher, and our elder, Liz was accustomed to being in charge of others. This was her first trip traveling with Josie or me.

Nevertheless she assured me, "I just wanted to go with the flow."

I asked Jenni the same question before we left, "How did you feel about going on this trip to Ireland?"

"We've traveled with our kids lots of times," she said. "It'll be a blast, especially all adults! I can help by navigating. I love maps and knowing about where I'm going."

I thought it was good to settle important roles at the beginning.

"Well, Josie will be the navigator," I said. "She'll sit in the front seat and direct me. Maybe you, Jen, can read about where we're going in the *Blue Guide* so you can tell us as we drive."

When Jenni is enthusiastic, sentences end with an exclamation point.

"Yeah, okay!" Jen said. "I love knowing stuff about where I'm going. I'll take lots of walks early wherever we are so I can ride in the car a long time. I like to walk around on the ground and just look at everything. Can we horseback ride like we did in Scotland? Plus it'll be fun for all of us to be together!"

Josie and I worked through winter, planning routes and arranging

lodgings. Our anticipation ran high. In addition, as our resident foodie, Josie was in charge of finding and choosing our dining.

"What were you thinking about how this would go before we left?" I asked her.

"Well, I thought Ireland would be beautiful, but not woo woo," Josie said. "I didn't think of it as the land of my ancestors, since I related myself to my Dad's side in Scotland. I was excited to travel and connect with Liz and Jenni on this first trip with them both, to say nothing of drinking a genuine Guinness!"

And she foreshadowed both of my sisters' extroversion after the first day of traveling, "My god, in the airport, Liz and Jenni will talk to anybody!"

Josie is on the quiet side with other people until she knows them well enough to have shared a Guinness or two. Then watch out, she'll dance on the tables.

I score high on the introverted scale. After a lifetime in a country that prizes extroversion, I have developed the performance art of appearing outgoing. While creativity and ideas fascinate me, people interest me more from a distance until I get to know them. However when someone becomes important to me I'm loyal and candid. With my tribe, I can become positively outgoing. I love to explore, and I especially enjoy traveling with Josie.

The barn at The Flax Cottage

CHAPTER I

ORIGINS

*The mammoths grazed on tundra grass before the trees
took root, and people followed with their fire and tools
by coast into the russet warmth of setting suns.
Here, eras of geology sit side by side –
ephemeral edges where the human dreams begin.*

~Leslie Lee, *Sacred Space*

I HAVE A LONGTIME INTEREST in how ancient languages evolved and migrated throughout the world. That has prompted an equal interest in the emerging field of genetic ancestry. Questions of how the data from the new technology compared to that of historical linguistics spurred me to test with the National Geographic/IBM Project on human genomes in the mid-1990s. The paper results of my maternal DNA ancestry listed letters and numbers on a matrix. The letters related to proteins in the genes, and the numbers indicated which genes in this segment under study had mutated. The mutations, natural changes over time in the genes, showed who was descended from whom. With this information, the project then mapped the lines of these mothers and their offspring, starting around fifty thousand years ago when they left Africa to cross the continents to their future homelands.

For years, after I was myself a mother, I felt the lines of our direct maternal ancestry pulling me to them. The magic words, *my mother's mother's, mother's mother…. back to the beginning of time*, was like clicking through a series of tiny gears in a complicated watch mechanism in my psyche. For me, this phenomenon centered not only on *who*, but as importantly, *where*. There are places in the world that make the hairs on my arms stand up with the feeling of a strong presence. It could be in a remote

canyon or in a church. I feel others overlaid like an invisible scent on the landscape. Who were they, these mothers I sensed? I was about to find out when the envelope from the National Geographic Genomic Project arrived. I ripped it open, found the map, the matrix, and our clan mother result. She was called *H*. Her line of children migrated in an arc over the Black Sea westward to Europe over thousands of years.

Would we be able to marry that data with what Liz knew historically about our family genealogy? Over the winter I asked about our family, and learned as much as I could about Ireland, the culture, mythology, history, and people. It shocked me how little I knew.

I embarrassed myself to discover my misperceptions about the meaning of the term *Scotch-Irish*. They were not Scots and Irish who had intermarried as I had naively imagined. No, they were enemies. The Scots were mostly Presbyterians who in the early sixteen hundreds had been granted land, called plantations, in the Province of Ulster, Northern Ireland by the British to colonize and subdue the Catholic natives. In Ireland, the Scotch-Irish are called Ulster-Scots. By the middle of the seventeenth century, one hundred thousand Scots lived in Ireland mainly working in weaving and milling. However, English economic sanctions in the eighteenth century and religious prosecution prompted the Ulster-Scots to look toward America. The Church of England, a combination of Catholic and Protestant practices designed to unify England, rankled the Presbyterian Ulster-Scots who refused to adopt the new church. For this, they were removed from government, civil, and military positions of power. The deep resentment felt by the Ulster-Scots for the English later fueled the armies of the American Revolution to victory against the British.

I dug into my references of Scotch-Irish relatives on our father's side named Nixon. In a document left by a descendant, the children and grandchildren teased the old-country grandmother every time she claimed her great-grandfather James Radcliffe Nixon was from Ballywellwell, Ireland. They howled with laughter because she pronounced it Bally-well-WELL, as in *well-WELL old chap*. In the 1950s her dutiful, dubious great-grandson wrote to Ireland asking about the town, but he was told it did not exist. Poor grandma. She must have been disappointed.

Liz told me she would look into it. She did a Google sounds-like search and came up with a townland, a collection of nearly a thousand acres, called Ballywillwill

near the town of Castlewellan in Northern Ireland. She called with the news. I smoothed out the map with the phone propped between my shoulder and ear. Liz was highly romantic and especially interested in this place because it was near the famed misty mountains of Mourne, the home of the Bronte sisters. I drew a thin line from the closest town, Castlewellan, out into the sea and wrote, *Nixon. Ballywillwill.* If we traveled near that territory, we would look into the history.

Reading on, I learned my fourth great-grandfather, James Radcliffe Nixon, arrived as a child on the ship, the Algernon, on the eighteenth of May 1811 in New York with his parents, George and Mary Radcliffe Nixon. This made me even more curious. What forces played in their immigration from Northern Ireland? Where was the home they were leaving forever? How and when did they make their way from New York to Michigan? How exactly did they relate to my well-known, beloved grandmother, Beryl Niles, in Petoskey, Michigan? This story of immigration is played out in the family histories of thousands of European-Americans, and is an important thread in the fabric of the making of America.

Then two things happened that connected us to the Republic of Ireland.

First, I left a message for Liz, "Do we have any native Irish? What country was our mother's mother from?"

I always thought my mother's mother was English. She was Episcopal, educated, accomplished, stern, proper. Certainly not Irish.

"Where was her soft-spoken, loving mother, Nellie Fisher, from? And her mother's mother?" I asked.

"Nellie thought of herself as English, thinking her father, William Fisher's mother's name was Douglas," Liz said when she called back. "I guess she only referred to the Puritans on her father's English side of the family, the Waites and the Howlands."

Then Liz told me, unbeknownst to Nellie, all four of Nellie's grandparents were born in Ireland. Her father's parents were born in Northern Ireland and her mother's parents were the Quinlans from County Cork. The Quinlan family origin was not important enough for her to mention. They had been sweeping their Irish ancestry under the British carpet for generations. It was hard for me to wait to learn more from Liz as she continued her search. She asked our oldest cousin to review a box of items our eldest aunt had given him. Sifting through the

ROADS BUILT BY 100 BC

ROADS IN THE 1700's

ICELINE

SCOTLAND

RATHLIN ISLAND

INISHOWEN

BUSHMILLS

DERRY

STRABANE

CARRICK-FERGUS

Killibegs

DONEGAL

NEWTOWN STEWART

LOUGH NEAGH

BELFAST

A3

ARMAGH

CASTLEWELLEN

NEWCASTLE

NIXON

BALLINA

SLIGO

ENNISKILLEN

CAVAN

DUNDALK

N61

ACHILL ISLAND

NEWPORT WESTPORT

DELPHI LODGE

KELLS

SLANE

DROGHEDA

Newgrange Knowth Dowth

NAVAN

TARA

MORNINGTON HOUSE

LEENANE

KILMAINE

CONG (TURIN CASTLE)

N55

TRIM

N4

M4

DUBLIN

CLIFDEN

MULLINGAR

GALWAY

ATHLONE

ENFIELD

M7

TULLAMORE

PORTLAOISE

M8

GORT

N18

ROSCREA

N7

DOOLIN

10,000 YA
ICE NORTH OF HERE

LAHINCH MOYHOUSE

ENNIS

N7

LIMERICK

ICE LINE

N9

KILRUSH

SHANNON R.

R691

KILKENNY

CASHEL TIPPERARY

R697

TRALEE

BOHERBUE

N20

FERMOY

WATERFORD

WEXFORD

DINGLE

MALLOW

KILARNEY

CORK

MACROOM

DUNGARVIN

YOUGHAL

Lee

SKIBBEREAN

KINSALE

bits and pieces, Liz came across an interesting scrap of paper. It was a corner of our great-great-great grandfather Patrick Quinlan's application to become a U.S. citizen dated 1853 in Dayton, Ohio. At that time he was migrating to Kalamazoo, Michigan with his wife and new baby who was born in Ohio. Patrick Quinlan was reconnecting with people who immigrated before him who had worked on the railways in County Cork, Ireland as well. The application stated he arrived on a ship sailing the last day of January 1849. The words haunted me, *"the last day in January 1849."* The transatlantic passage took about twelve weeks on an old wooden sailing ship. It was during the potato famine era in Ireland. To sail across the ocean in mid-winter, they must have been mortally desperate.

The search was stirring a range of emotions as I sat in my Michigan home. Turning my head, I watched the howling snow in wind fly off the wave tops across Lake Michigan beat on my windows. I sensed my ancestors' determination to stay alive under such horrendous conditions, and the direct, unbroken connection to *our mother's, mother's mother, and back to the beginning of time.* My skin electrified as I thought of the traits and habits for successful childrearing and survival that was passed down to me from them. My head dropped as I choked back humbled, grateful tears.

The genetic genealogy revolution was just taking off in 1996 as technology advanced and public awareness grew. Research on my genetics background continued arriving by mail through Family Tree DNA, my new testing service. They sent me a notice that technology had progressed sufficiently to more closely identify segments of the H maternal line. We four sisters were H3, a line found in Ireland between six and eight thousand years ago. Indigenous Irish. Whoa. Now I was really interested in traveling in the Republic of Ireland.

Liz set off to explore shipping records and found a listing for Patrick Quinlan and Ellen Dineen from Boherbue, Ireland. Could they be our ancestors? By phone, we arranged to visit those local parish records in County Cork near the town of Mallow. I lifted an antique map of Ireland off the wall. With my finger and my imagination I traced the orchard-lined roads around Mallow imagining the women who came before me walking there in romantic sounding Duhollow. I thought of their qualities, their liveliness of spirit, and the spark they passed down to us. Soon I'd be tracing their actual footsteps.

(174) PORTAL TOMBS OR DOLMENS

5000 YEARS AGO

IN ULSTER LEINSTER N. MUNSTER

PROVINCE OF ULSTER

INSIDE COURT TOMBS: MIX OF CREMATION AND INHUMATION, GRAVE GOODS, POTS, AXE HEADS

6000 YEARS AGO

FOUND ACROSS NORTHERN THIRD.

PROVINCE OF CONNACHT

INSIDE WEDGE TOMBS: BEAKER POTTERY, ARROW-HEADS, V-BUTTONS

4300-4000 YEARS AGO

METAL WORKING PEOPLE

(390) COURT TOMBS

EAST FACING

SO-CALLED "PASSAGE TOMBS"

PROVINCE OF LEINSTER

(230)

WEDGE TOMBS (500)

WESTERN DISTRIBUTION: SW MUNSTER, N. MUNSTER, CO'S MAYO, SLIGO & DONEGAL

6000 YEARS AGO

MEGALITHIC ASTRONOMICAL RITUAL CENTER-TEMPLES

SURROUNDED BY DECORATED-INSCRIBED CURBSTONES

CREMATIONS BROUGHT TO THE SITES.

SIMILAR DISTRIBUTION AS PORTAL TOMBS, ON HILLTOPS

LINKARDSTOWN-TYPE CIST OR FLAT BURIAL

5600-5300 YEARS AGO

INSIDE: FLEXED INHUMATION, LONE MALES, WITH PERSONAL ITEMS,

PROVINCE OF MUNSTER

1. COURT TOMBS (390)
2. PORTAL TOMBS (174)
3. "PASSAGE TOMBS" (230)
4. LINKARDSTOWN-TYPE (?)
5. WEDGE TOMBS (500)

TOMB TYPES

CHAPTER II

EARLY IRELAND

Impenetrable ice, ten thousand years ago,
a mile above the lake it left in its retreat,
inscribed a polished passage on the former bed
of ocean life still etched upon this stony floor,
and deeper still, carved lakes that filled with glacial melt.

~Leslie Lee, *Sacred Space*

AS I CURLED UP SURROUNDED BY BOOKS, maps, and telephone, fall turned to winter. For sixteen years, I'd lived in northern Michigan on the shore of the big lake in the small town where I raised my family. The fire crackled. Snow-blown waves pounded outside my window. I studied.

I didn't know much and the more I learned, the more I realized I didn't know. Still, I had so many questions. Where had the Irish people come from? What was a Celt? How was I supposed to pronounce the word Celtic? How does Celtic relate to Gaelic? What happened to create so much discord in Ireland and Northern Ireland? What was the potato famine? Why have I always been embarrassed by leprechauns? It must be I felt the shame of being reduced to an unflattering comical character. That's just the beginning.

Understanding the beginning of time and people in Ireland is complex. If my general ignorance weren't enough, in the past twenty years we've been in the middle of a quiet revolution that is daily rewriting world history, anthropology, and medicine. As new information and data churn from the genetic labs, regularly I have to eat my words, redraw my maps, and re-chart the graphs.

It's important to realize human history in the broader context of time, and it makes me smile at the manipulative, political side of human nature to have used it so effectively so early. Astronomer Galileo was thrown into prison in the early 1600s for arguing the Earth was not the center of the universe. It took people no time at all to proselytize their beliefs, market their wares, and influence others' behavior using the written word. Interestingly, though history doesn't always match with modern knowledge, mythology often does. I was surprised to discover that climatic events were regularly represented in Irish mythology.

What was the land like at the dawn of modern humans? Imagine a blank sheet of ice covering the northern hemisphere to around the fiftieth parallel. South of its boundary existed polar desert for hundreds of miles. South of that polar desert stretched a giant swath of tundra, or grassy steppe, from east to west from Mongolia to the Balkans like a conveyor belt for large game and the humans who hunted them. Three times in fifty thousand years advancing glaciers forced entire populations into pockets of refuge before warming climates melted receding glaciers into lakes and rivers, once again creating the life-giving steppes. During warm times the people moved north into Britain, Ireland, Norway, and along the northern coastlines. Masses of people grouped up, hunted, interbred, and retreated to refuges when the glaciers returned. They continued to interbreed and migrate in complicated patterns of coming together and separating. One can visualize not a family tree, but a great river delta of crisscrossing ancestries.

These were the hunter-gatherers of the Mesolithic Era, and they formed the bedrock genes in Eurasia and Western Europe referred to as Basal Eurasians. The ice age of twenty thousand years ago created so much polar ice that ocean levels dropped. Any artifacts of earlier ice ages would be under water of that now submerged coastline. When it was cold and dry, the English Channel and the Celtic Sea were frozen land across which humans and game traveled on one side or the other of the single Rhine-Thames River. Genetic echoes of this division are seen in inhabitants of East Coast England differing from those who arrived in West England, West Scotland, and Ireland on the southwest side of the great river.

In times of glacial advance, the most western of these hunter-gatherers took refuge in the Basque territory on the northern border of what are now Spain and France. Experts call it the Franco-Cantabrian refuge. My direct

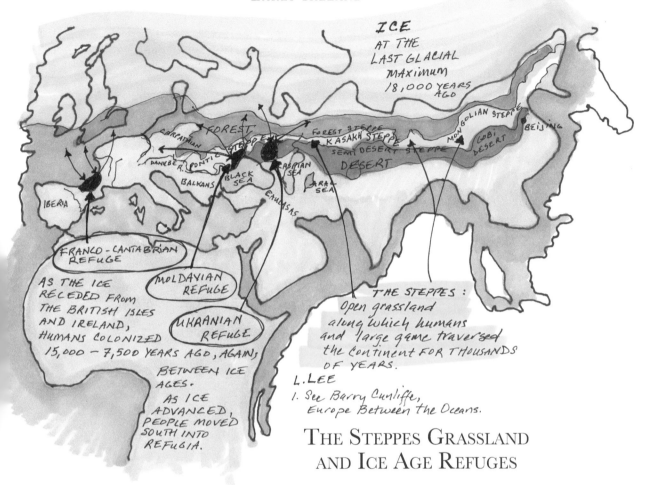

**THE STEPPES GRASSLAND
AND ICE AGE REFUGES**

maternal line, H3, likely arose there or in Sardinia. Following the last great freeze of the Younger Dryas that ended eleven thousand, five hundred years ago the world entered a warming trend. When times warmed H3's daughter's lineage moved north with the male lineage of hunter-gatherers along coastlines and up river valleys into Ireland, the British Isles, and Norway to reclaim lands their ancestors may have known. Archeological evidence places people in Ireland nine thousand years ago. It wasn't long before farmers from Anatolia and the Levant were on the move west along the Mediterranean Sea reaching Western Europe, Sardinia, and the Isles eight thousand years ago. Within a thousand years their farming genes mixed with those of the early hunter-gatherers.

The seas rose creating the British Isles and Ireland as separate from the continent for the last time around seven thousand five hundred years ago.

Authors William Ryan and Walter Pitman's research in their book, *Noah's Flood*, told of rising sea levels that broke through the Bosporus into the Black Sea creating the epic flood of Noah and Gilgamesh. The flow of saltwater pouring into the freshwater lake was two hundred times the amount of water that flows over Niagara Falls every day. This caused the level of the lake-sea to rise six inches a day without pause. Since the time of that research, author David Anthony explained a theory in his book *The Horse, The Wheel, and Language.* He wrote that meltwater from receding glaciers flowed into the Caspian Sea creating an enormous lake to the north, and finally overflowing its southwestern border into the Black Sea caused it to rise and flow out the Bosporous into the Aegean Sea.

Whichever version is more accurate, all of the people living on the banks of the Black Sea needed to move away from the shorelines. In order to survive, all life needed to move away or up the Rivers Dnieper, Dniester, and the Danube to the north in a great diaspora.

I'm still trying to figure out which people built the great so-called Irish passage "tombs" Newgrange, Knowth, Dowth, and Loughcrew. These older-than-the-pyramids constructions were gigantic mounds of dry laid stone. They seem to me to be ceremonial centers rather than tombs. Inside were chambers for ceremonies and rituals conducted by the druids to ensure bountiful harvests and fertility. Were they early farmers who share so much of their genetic ancestry with Sardinians who then mixed with Mesolithic era hunter-gatherers as they moved north into Ireland? Many Sardinians were women of the H3 line and they traveled with the hunter-gathers of the G2 and I Ydna lines. Or were they a later wave of farmers who also marked their territory with dolman style megaliths?

I wondered especially about the Celts and who they were. I learned they were not the Swiss Halstatt culture of the Iron Age as some historians had thought, but were earlier Bronze Age warrior-traders of five thousand years ago from the Pontic Steppe north of the Black Sea that geneticists have since identified.

To understand the Celts, or Gaels, it is important to understand a little about male DNA. Geneticists examine the Y chromosome of men to measure the distance between mutations to determine the passage of time. It's a clock. It measures time and marks it with a mutation. Y is the male line sex chromosome men carry in their genes. Men also carry the X chromosome of the maternal line, or mitochondrial

line often referred to as MT DNA. However, men cannot pass down MT DNA. Only women can pass along mitochondrial DNA to their offspring. The mutations themselves are a roadmap of ancestry. What confuses me is the changing nomenclature by scientists for male ancestral lines. This is important only for those people who have an old DNA test with old nomenclature that they want to compare. At first the geneticists named them with letters and numbers, and then they changed them.

The most successful male line in the British Isles and Ireland was called R1B1. It was called the Atlantic Modal Haplotype, or L-23 as well. As with H on the female side, R1B1 came to dominate the genetic pool.

Clan mother H, or Helena, remained one of the bedrock maternal genetic lines. Maternal DNA lines are stable, ancient, and regional. The AMH R1B1 men of five thousand years ago wiped out nearly all of the extant hunter-gatherer, Basal European and farming genes of the men before them. Most of the G2 and I men were no more. This is possible with male genes simply because men can procreate many times over with many women over the course of a long life. Women cannot because of the time needed to carry a baby to term. So if male lines dominate a culture, they will also dominate the male offspring.

This is what happened with the Bronze Age R1B1 men from the steppes. These nomadic herders of cattle domesticated the horse, perfected the wheel and cart, and formed an aristocratic warrior society. They were on the move west until they could travel west no further, to Ireland five thousand years ago. They brought horses, metalworking, and the Indo-European language.

They brought their genes, Celtic genes. These later arrivals to Ireland may have been the builders of the magnificent portal tombs. Or they may have arrived with a later group, also related, four thousand five hundred years ago known as the Bell Beaker people from Iberia.

Geneticist David Reich tells us in *Who We Are And How We Got Here* that the DNA of Irish men is ten percent first farmers and a whopping ninety percent Bell Beaker people. Who were they? I turned to Barry Cunliffe's *Oxford Illustrated History of Prehistoric Europe* to find out. It seems they were newcomers of an entirely different sort. When they arrived five thousand years ago they dominated the existing communal, female-worshipping, megalith-building, place-based early farming communities of Ireland.

Imagine these strange young seafaring men in the local harbor coming ashore on horses. With alcohol. They wore colorful, corded, status belts with bone rings, copper ornaments, bronze daggers, and archery equipment. They were brash, martial, and ostentatious. By the time they reached Ireland, they had influenced the maritime and riverine cultures they passed through from the Danube to Spain. Some of those cultures resisted them and others fell sway to their ways. In Ireland the people learned copper and gold metallurgy from them, but did not adopt their drinking and individualistic burial practices which was to bury elite men each in their own grave with weapons and drinking jar at hand. All the Bell Beaker people had the DNA of the Corded Ware Steppes culture. Clearly they had their way with women. They were the Celts.

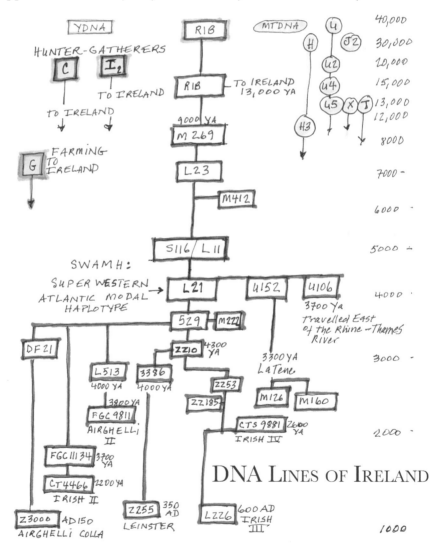

DNA Lines of Ireland

TERRITORIES, POPULATION GROUPS, AND DNA CIRCA AD 1000

FOR SCHOLARSHIP SEE:
MacLysaght, Edward, The Surnames of Ireland
FamilyTreedna.com and
wikipedia

SNP M222 | NW IRISH
SON OF NIALL OF THE NINE HOSTAGES
O'NEILL
TIR CONAILL: O'Gallaghers, O'Donnell
O'Boyles, O'Doherty
TIR EOGHAIN: BRADLEY, DEVLIN,
DONNELLY, GORMLEY, McCaul
CAMPBELL, McLAUGHLIN, O'KANE, QUIN
ETC.

222

CENÉL CONAILL
NORTHERN UÍ NÉILL
AILECH
222
TIR CHONAILL
222
TIR EOGHAIN
CENEL EOGHAIN
AIRGIALLA
(ORGHIALLA)
(ORIEL)
Z 3000

DÁL RIATA
McDONNELL

ULIAD
DOWNPATRICK
DÁL FIATACH

uí BRIUIN BRÉIFNE
McDonald
CLOGHER
McDonald
Mc MAHON
McGuire
Carroll
McKenna

AIRGIALLA
Z 3000
McDonald
MacMahon
McGuire
Carroll
McKenna
etc.

Dal Fiatach
Dun Leavy
Haughey
McGuinness
McCartan
etc.

UÍ FIACHRACH
O'HARA
uí BRIUIN AI
O'MALLEY
IAR CONNACHT

SILMURRAY:
O'CONNOR

CONNACHT
SÍOL MUIREADHAIGH
uí BRIUIN
O'KELLY
SÍOL ANMCHADHA
uí MÁINE

SOUTHERN UÍ NÉILL
KNOWTH
LOEGAIRE TARA
BREGA
LAGORE
CAIRBRE
O'REILLY
uí FAELAN | NAAS CUAN
uí DÚLAINGE
uí CANCHON
LEINSTER
Z 255
LAIGIN
Z 255

uí BRIUIN:
O'CONNOR, O'REILLY, HYNES,
FLYNN, McGOVERN, McMANUS
O'ROURKE, etc.

CORCA MUAD
TUATHMHUMHAN
(THOMOND)
CORCA BAISCIND
LYNCH
DÉISI
DAL CAIS
226
MUSCRIGE TIRE
EILE
uí FAILGE
LOIGIS
OSRAIGE
O'Brennan
uí BANCHE
uí DRONA
uí ENACHGLAID
KAVANAUGH
uí CHENNSELAIG

THE LEINSTER MODAL
Z 255
O'Byrne
Murphy
Ryan
Kelly
Kavanaugh
Donohoe
McEvoy
Kinsella
etc.

4466 | IRISH TYPE II
EOGHANACHT:
SON OF OILIOLL
OLUM AND
DESCENDANTS—
CAISIL AND RATHLIND
= IRISH TYPE II | 4466
O'Sullivans
O'Keefes
O'Mahoney
O'McCarthy
O'Donovan
of Corca Laidhe
etc.

uí FIDGENTI | 4466
CIARRAIGE LUACHRA
EOGHANACHT
MUNSTER
MAC CARHAIGH
CORCA DUIBHNE
EÓGANACHT GLENNAMAIN
DEASMHUMHAN
O'DONOGHUE
MUSCRAIDHE
(O'LEARY)
LOCHA LÉIN
O'SULLIVAN MOR
CORCA LOIGDE
EÓGANACHT RATHLIN
MAHONEY
O'DONOVAN
O'DRISCOLL

EOGHANACHT CAISIL
O'CALLAGHAN
CASHEL
DÉSI MUMAN
uí LIATHÁIN

uí DRONA
KAVANAUGH
uí CHENNSELAIG

ANCIENT TERRITORIES OF IRELAND

IRISH TYPE III
Dál gCais | 226
O'Brien, McGraw
MacMahon, O'Casey, etc.

& | POPULATION GROUPS | & | DNA
Clann (children)   Corca (race)
Dal (tribe)   Tuaithe (people)

Irish Mythology

We European-Americans don't have much mythology to anchor ourselves to the past unlike people of the old world who are raised with these stories from the time they are children. The legend of Paul Bunyan was scarcely two hundred years ago. Our mythology isn't older than this. Native American mythology is rich and varied, but we newcomers aren't usually taught that. Learning the rudiments of the stories of Ireland that stretched far before modern history was yet another fundamental aspect of traveling to Ireland to enrich my stay. Irish mythology reflects geological advances, retreats, and floods, and the invasions of people surprisingly well. Invasion, to me, means military conquering of established inhabitants. But in the context of the mythology, an invasion may just as easily mean a migrating population.

The Book of Invasions, an oral history, also known as *Lebor Gabala Erenn,* records the six sets of peoples and events that took place from the beginning of time in Ireland to the Middle Ages. Oral history was a form of passing knowledge from one generation to the next without losing the power of the information, like trade secrets of today. The recipients of this knowledge were called Senchas and the great Book of Knowledge was called En Senchus Mor. This druidic class of storytellers told the mythology, history, genealogy, religious rituals, Brehon laws, herbs and medicine, and elements of the natural world. These professional storytellers were trained for years until every word was memorized. Then they went out to teach and practice their craft.

I have assigned the dates after reading and reasoning for my best guesses based on genetics, archeology, and changes in the climate. The following paragraphs summarize elements of the six invasions:

Fomorians. Nine thousand years ago. Forever.

Whether peaceful arrivals or not, later invaders fought the giant sea pirates, the Fomorians, whose strongholds were the Tory Islands nine miles off County Donegal. They were said to have lived forever in the north. I wondered

which genetic population they may have been. Were they possibly the earliest hunter-gatherers of a Y DNA that no longer exists? Were they early Norsemen? Or did they simply represent the forces of darkness for all who followed? Two distinct early stone tool types, microliths, and butt and distally trimmed blades dating to nine thousand years ago, were found in the north near Derry by archeologists.

1ST CESAIR. SEVEN THOUSAND FIVE HUNDRED YEARS AGO.

The first of six invasions traditionally listed is Cesair, a queen, and daughter of Noah, who escaped just ahead of the rising flood landing in Bantry Bay in County Cork. To me, this may refer to Noah's flood seven thousand five hundred years ago when the salt water of the Mediterranean broke through the Bosporus to raise the former freshwater lake, now the Black Sea, to current sea level. Or, if Cesair was sojourning in the Iberian refuge, it may have referred to the rising glacial meltwater of the Irish Sea between seventy-five hundred and six thousand years ago before which the Islands were part of the continent. Either way, it places her in Ireland in the same timeframe. I imagine her to be clan mother, U4, Ursula, or H, Helena, genetically.

2ND PARTHALON. SEVEN THOUSAND YEARS AGO.

The second invasion was of the Parthelonians who seem to me to match up with the early farmers. Geneticists identify the farming men as G2 and I2, and the women as H1, H3, U5, and V. But now the ancient DNA of G men in Ireland represent only one percent of the population today. These, having merged with existing hunter-gathering populations, would have been the builders of the megaliths of Newgrange, Knowth, Dowth and Loughcrew.

Parthalon arrived from the east along the Mediterranean Sea landing near Donegal. The myth relates that Parthalon introduced agriculture, married Dealgnaid, had four sons, and divided Ireland in four parts. He established just laws regarding fostering children, cauldron making, and drinking ale. The Parthalonians established rules around hospitality.

Archeological remains of domesticated ox were found on Dalkey Island off Dublin. They were thought to have sheep, goats and cattle. They cleared forests for farming and pasturage so much so that more than eighteen thousand polished stone axes were found in Ireland. Pollen records show they grew cereals. Excavations at Ceide Fields in County Mayo showed fields marked by court tombs and portal tombs experts believe marked the family territories as a deed of ownership.

They flourished for a long time, reaching a population of nine thousand before they all died in the same week of May.

Why did they die so suddenly? The best answer was that a comet struck close enough to have caused a form of winter. Scientists who study tree rings can see the month a comet obliterates the light and ends growth and can tell how long it lasts. Or, possibly, a visitor brought an extremely virulent plague.

3ᴿᴰ NEMED. SIX THOUSAND YEARS AGO.

Nemed, a son of Noah, left his Scythian home with his wife, Macha, and their four sons and wives. They arrived soon after the plague. The reference to the Scythians may link the Nemedians to an early wave of Corded Ware pottery people from the Pontic Steppe invaders. These were R1b1 men, also known as the Yamnaya, who in the future overwhelmed the earlier male genetic lines. The DNA of the women most closely associated with these men were H, U5, T2, and T1 in order of diminishing percentages. To make these designations seem more like the real women they were, geneticist Bryan Sykes called them Helena, Ursula 5, Tara 2, and Tara 1.

The Nemedians settled in Armagh, meaning Macha's hill, where they built a fortress, and in County Antrim where they built a second fortress. Their chief druid, Mide, for whom County Meath is named, lit the first ceremonial fire at Uisneach that blazed for seven years. This was the site, the center or naval of their world, from which the kings lit their own fires. That the Nemedians cleared fields in dense forests may relate to opening up pasturage for cattle and horses if they were the same herders of the Corded Ware pottery heritage from the Steppes.

The mythology claims after many battles the Nemedians were enslaved by the Fomorians. Or they were made their vassals. This seems so unlikely to me if these warriors were to go on to take over the male DNA of the Isles and had the benefit of the horses, wagons, and possibly chariots. These Nemedians may have been earlier R1B1 Yamnaya entrants to Ireland before their relatives arrived en masse in a later invasion. Myth says some escaped to Greece, some say to Belgium, to become the ancestors of the Fir Bolg, and some escaped to the North of Britain to become the Tuatha de Danaan. They will return.

4ᵀᴴ FIR BOLG. FIVE THOUSAND YEARS AGO.

Myths claim the Fir Bolg arrived in Malahide Bay near Dublin during Lughnasa, the first of August, many generations after the Nemedians scattered. They had escaped slavery from Belgium or Greece where they labored hauling dirt in leather bags by turning the bags into boats. King Eochaid MacAirt and his wife Tailtiu established a peaceable kingdom dividing Ireland in four parts for their sons. Myth compiler, Lady Gregory, said they had no law but love, no religion, and that there was peace and plenty. Interestingly, there is no mention of Fomorians during the reign of the Fir Bolg. Had they forged an alliance or treaty? Is it possible the Fir Bolg are related to the archeologically known Bell Beaker folk of Iberia and the Netherlands? By four thousand years ago, many forests had been opened up for farming and pasturage to graze cows, horses, and wool bearing sheep.

5ᵀᴴ TUATHA DE DANAAN. FOUR THOUSAND FIVE HUNDRED YEARS AGO.

These are the tribes of the god of three skills. Tuatha means tribes; Danaan means *of Anan*. Arriving in a dark cloud before Beltine, the first of May, they settled on a mountain in the west. The dark cloud may relate to the catastrophic eruption of the volcano Hekla 4 four thousand years ago, or Santorini one thousand years later.

Descended from Nemedians who escaped north, they were healers, masters of the arts, of smithcraft, poetry, and song. A white cow was their goddess and the warrior, Lug, their god. They defeated the Fir Bolg and Fomorians in epic battles at Mag Tuired to win the right to rule Ireland at Tara. Three sons of Dagda divided Ireland and married three goddesses who excelled in a long list of arts and skills. They then built a great fort at Ailech in County Donegal at Inishowen Head. (This became the seat of the Ui Neill until it was seized in AD 425.)

The Tuatha de Danaan ruled for thousands of years until the arrival of the Milesians who defeated them. However, the Tuatha de Danaan was a magical race of ever-living beings. The Milesians and they divided the world in two, one above ground for the Milesians. The other world below was an idyllic, ageless place of beauty which the Tuatha de Danaan thereafter were forced to inhabit. The underground world was accessed by sidhs, or fairy mounds.

Celtic metalwork and design began in the trading Hallstatt Culture north and east of the Austrian Alps in the early Iron Age two thousand nine hundred years ago. The artistic style culminated in the breathtaking bronze, silver, and gold work of the La Tene style people who flourished between two thousand five hundred to two thousand fifty years ago. Their intricate designs are considered the epitome of Celtic art.

Were these cultures the origin of the Tuatha de Danaan? Are they also R1B1 Yamnaya descendants who contributed to the overwhelming R1B1 male gene pool of the British Isles and Ireland?

6ᴛʜ MILESIANS. THREE THOUSAND FIVE HUNDRED YEARS AGO.

It seems clear that everything changed dramatically after the arrival of the Milesians. These, then, were the final wave of people from the Steppes, the Bronze Age warriors of the Corded Ware pottery heritage. If the Tuatha de Danaan ruled for thousands of years, and the Milesians were the last invaders or arrivals, then I wondered if the Milesians may be Bell Beaker people of R1B1 who had settled in Spain. Not the earlier Fir Bolg from Belgium, but those from Iberia from four thousand five hundred years ago.

Or the Milesians may have been a different group of people arriving in Ireland from the Basque Refuge in Spain, or Iberia.

Mil Espaine, *a soldier of Spain*, claimed origins from Noah, and Scythia as well. He was married to Scota, a noble Irishwoman, with whom they had sons. He died in Spain, but knew they were to go to Ireland from a druid, even though they had never seen it. A son built a high tower from which he glimpsed a shore of the land of the oracle. After reaching Ireland, he was treacherously killed on the way to his ship after meeting three kings of the Tuatha de Danaan at Ailech, in Derry.

The sons of Mil returned to conquer Ireland. They landed at Inber Scene to defeat the Tuatha de Danaan. After meeting three kings at Tara, they were tricked into leaving Ireland. A brewing storm threatened to wreck their ships, but they were saved by the poet Amergin who recited a poem that stilled the waters. Once again on Irish soil his brother, Eremon, led the remaining brothers around Ireland in a sunwise turn to bring them luck to the Boyne River estuary. A sunwise turn is accomplished by keeping the object to the right of the person as he or she moves in a circle around the object, the well, the house, or the world. Meeting the Tuatha de Danaan at Tailtiu (Teltown in County Meath) and Druim Ligen (near Rapoe, County Donegal) they were soon crushed. Once again, Ireland was divided among them with the widow of Mil, Scota, naming all the Irish people the Scoti.

As a side note, a thousand years later a large group of Irish people migrated to nearby Alba. The inhabitants in Alba referred to these newcomers as the Scoti. After hundreds of years of intermarrying all of Alba came to be called Scotland.

	60 - 40 KYA	40 - 20 KYA	20 - 15 KYA	15,000 - 10,000 ya
NOTES / Myth	700,000 - 200,000 ya super archaic humans — "Ghost" DNA	Prehistoric humans relate distance to the time it takes to get there. Hunter-gatherers expanded into new territory at the rate of 2-3 kilometers/year.	(1st) 14,000ya Cesair arrives in Ireland	
DNA	Neanderthals and non-Africans interbreed. 50-40 Kya. Denisovians interbreed with non-African San. Move East.	Hunter Gatherers from East to Western Europe. (WHG) 39kya Neanderthals are extinct. R1B1 YDNA, + ←MtDNA U5, N. (Ursula) to Europe YDNA-I.J. to G2, C1	Early people blend in the Franco-Cantabrian refuge - Basque. H (Helena) in Europe 25,000 ya.	I2 YDNA and U5 in Europe R1B9 , R1B14. 15Kya Hunter-gatherer genes from SE and East blend with European H-Gs. Mtdna H3 arises from within Europe, possibly Sardinia. Mtdna-H in Western Europe.
Culture	A group of San people leave Africa. Begin to populate the non-African world. 60kya 40 Kya Aurignacian Culture.	35 Kya - 22Kya Gravettian Culture. Chauvet Cave paintings, Magdalenian Culture in SW France female worship, sewing needles used. 26 kya - Solutrean Culture	16-13 Kya Older Dryas period of very cold climate send Northern people into refugia. 15kya - Only Ice in Britain. 14 Kya - Sudden warming = floods. 11 Kya - Britain repopulates, as does N. Europe. People and game flow East to West. FARMING BEGINS IN NEAR EAST	
Nature / Climate	UPPER PALEOLITHIC ERA/AGE TO 10,000 ya.	39kya Campi Flegri Naples erupts. Ash over Pontic Steppe Maximum ice pushes South	LGM - Last Glacial Maximum Western Europeans move South to the Franco-Cantabrian Refuge (Basque) Last Glacial Maximum 25-15 Kya UPPER PALEOLITHIC AGE	In Ireland, grassland, deer, H-G, fishing. "younger dryas" 13kya-12 kya - quick freez 14,000ya - Sudden Warmth - Flood FLOOD Alpine Ice melts Very cold 16 kya - 13 kya Older Dryas 50 - 10 KYA WARMING

L. LEE

9000ya: Irish myth
of Fomorians → the
giants from the North
future invaders battled.

7500 YA ⚊ or 14,000 ya
Ireland—
(1st) invasion:
CESAIR
(2nd) invasion:
~~7500~~ 7500 YA – 6500 ya
Parthalon:
early farmers

West Eurasian populations
blend. American Indians
retain ⅓ of This ancestry
as They migrate East.

YDNA G2a,
mtdna X2 arrived with
early farmers.

YDNA- R1B1 in Franco-
Cantabrian refuge, and
migrating as H-G to England
and Ireland when Ice allows.

MTDNA HELENA
(H) to Ireland

YDNA G2a
I, I2

Evidence of first people
in Ireland. Hunter-gathers.

West Eurasian populations
collapse into each other
blending DNA.

Black Sea
(from Ukraine)
on The Pontic Steppes,
Anatolian Farmers
+ Hunter gatherers
= Corded Ware pottery,
people of Pontic Steppes
developing wheeled carts,
cattle herding, domesticating
horses = Yamnaya.

First Farmers
from Mediterranean Route
to Sardinia, Ireland.

.Danube
Linear band Ceramic
~~7500~~ 7500-6500 ya
Seafaring.
Sheep in Italy

7000 ya:
Linen weaving
Copper and
gold ornaments.

Flint and
obsidean tools.

HOLOCENE EPOCH "COMPLETELY NEW"

Mammoth habitat of
grasslands are replaced
by Woodlands in Ireland.

Last glacier.
Black
Sea
Flood.

HEKLA
Icelandic ERUPTS IN
7600 YA
Hazel, pine, Elm, oak
to Ireland. FLOOD

FLOODING
Ice between Ireland
& Britain
FLOOD
6500

MESOLITHIC ERA

10 – 9000 YA	9000 – 8000 YA	8000 – 7000 YA

see Reich, David, Oppenheimer, Steven   Thank you, L. Lee
Sykes, Bryan

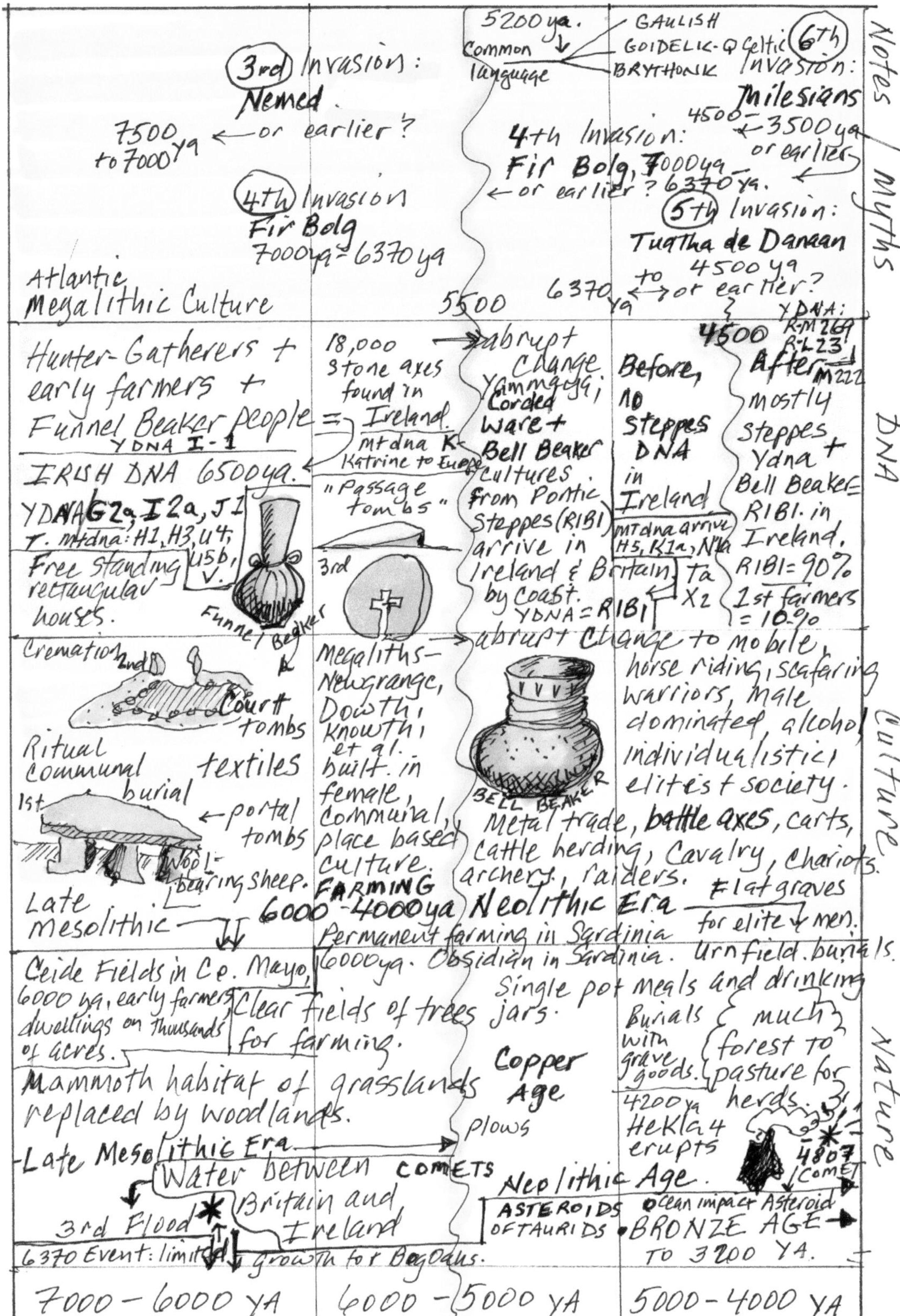

5200 ya. | GAULISH
Common language → | GOIDELIC-Q Celtic
| BRYTHONIC

(6th) Invasion:
Milesians
4500 ← 3500 ya
or earlier?

(3rd) Invasion:
Nemed.
7500 to 7000 ya ← or earlier?

4th Invasion:
Fir Bolg, 7000 ya.
← or earlier? 6370 ya.

(4th) Invasion
Fir Bolg
7000 ya – 6370 ya

(5th) Invasion:
Tuatha de Danaan
6370 ya ← to 4500 ya or earlier?

Atlantic Megalithic Culture   5500

4500   Y DNA: R-M269 R-L23 M222

Column 1 (7000 – 6000 YA)

Hunter-Gatherers + early farmers + Funnel Beaker people = Y DNA I-1

IRISH DNA 6500 ya.
Y DNA G2a, I2a, J1 T. mtdna: H1, H3, u4, u5b, V.
Free standing rectangular houses.

Cremation 2nd
Court tombs
Ritual communal textiles
1st burial
← portal tombs
Wool-bearing sheep.
Late Mesolithic

Ceide Fields in Co. Mayo, 6000 ya, early farmers dwellings on thousands of acres.
Mammoth habitat of grasslands replaced by woodlands.
- Late Mesolithic Era.
3rd Flood ✱
6370 Event: limited growth for Bog Oaks.

7000 – 6000 YA

Column 2 (6000 – 5000 YA)

18,000 stone axes found in Ireland.
mtdna K Katrine to Europe
"Passage tombs"
3rd

Megaliths – Newgrange, Dowth, Knowth, et al. built in female communal, place based culture.
FARMING 6000 – 4000 ya
Clear fields of trees for farming.

Water between Britain and Ireland
COMETS
ASTEROIDS OF TAURIDS
6000 – 5000 YA

Column 3 (center)

abrupt change Yamnaya, Corded Ware + Bell Beaker cultures from Pontic Steppes (R1B1) arrive in Ireland & Britain by coast. Y DNA = R1B1

abrupt change to mobile, horse riding, seafaring warriors, male dominated, alcohol, individualistic, elites + society.
Metal trade, battle axes, carts, cattle herding, cavalry, chariots, archery, raiders. Flat graves for elite + men.

BELL BEAKER

Permanent farming in Sardinia. 6000 ya. Obsidian in Sardinia. Single pot meals and drinking jars.
Copper Age
Plows
Neolithic Age.
Ocean impact Asteroid
BRONZE AGE →
TO 3200 YA.

5000 – 4000 YA

Column 4 (5000 – 4000 YA)

Before, no steppes DNA in Ireland
mtdna arrive H5, K1a, N1a Ta X2

After, mostly steppes Ydna + Bell Beaker R1B1. in Ireland. R1B1 = 90% 1st farmers = 10%

Urnfield burials. Burials with grave goods.
4200 ya Hekla 4 erupts
4807 / COMET
forest to pasture for herds.

Notes/Myths

4500 ya to now Milesians "Invasion." Q-Celtic, goidelic

Ulster Cycle (or Red Branch) AD 100 of heroic legends of Ulster. Cú Chulainn and the Cattle Raid of Cooley. (Táin Bó Cúailnge). →

Tara — Fenian Cycle → Fionn and Diarmuid, Salmon of Knowledge. Ossian tales. →

DNA

Mtdna - X2, H5, K1a, N1a, Ta, X2 female dna remains stable. The women stay with the land, as the YDNA changes.

YDNA - R1B1 - L.11 Bronze Age Steppes with R1B1 L-21-(m222)(m269) soon become 80% of Irish men dna.

Mtdna H, V, J, T, u, K. recent haplogroup R. now 90% of Mtdna.

M269 = R1b1a1a2 9000-4500 ya → L23 to Ireland, L 23 → L 21 → M222 = UiNiell, Connachta, Uí Bruin, Ui Fiachrach. L159.2 = Kings of Leinster, & Laigin. R-L226 = Irish type III Dálcais. R-L371 = "Welsh modal" Kings and Princes. H1 + H3 mtdna = 22.5% in Ireland.

M269 L23 Ydna — 450 AD L 21 (m222) Niall of ancestor the of the Nine UiNiell in Hostages. NW Ireland. 25% of

H1 + H3 mtdna = 22.5% in Ireland.

people in NW are descended from him

Culture

Stonehenge built. Úne tice Culture 4300-3600 ya. Major metal industry, trade goods, swords developed in Alpine region - 3500 ya.

Chariots in Europe.

Marked difference in how people viewed death and after-life in Urnfield Culture.

Late Bronze Age Collapse of Cultures: 3200 ya Mycenea, in By failed Greece, destroyed. Sea Egypt, Hitittes under attack, Levant devasted.

3300 ya - Surge in Bronze working in Urnfield Europe/Steppes, Caucasus. Hill forts, Iran flat cemeteries.

← Ulster Cycle →

AD 300 St. Fall of Emain Patrick/ macha Christianity 2600-2400 arrives

Hallstatt Culture in Ireland AD 432

LaTene Style, AD 500, Dark Ages for Ireland

Nature

Classic Bronze Age Plague 3900 ya Hekla (HSV) Erupts

Track building for Carts.

3800 ya 3642 →

✱ 4350 Non-volcanic event, Aegean 3100 ya Hekla 3 Erupts catastrophically causing 18 years of dark. Tree rings show NO GROWTH for 3 years. Stunted growth for 15.

← Santorini erupts

Late Bronze 2600 ya Age

IRON AGE →

Plague? • 94 BC- Central post at Navan Fort was felled.

Iron Age

Irish roads built. Barrows & ditches forts. AD ✱ 540 Event that severely limited Oak growth. AD 500 - AD 1000

1 BC | AD 1

4000 — 3000 ya	3000 — 2000 ya	2000 — 1000 ya

L. Lee

23

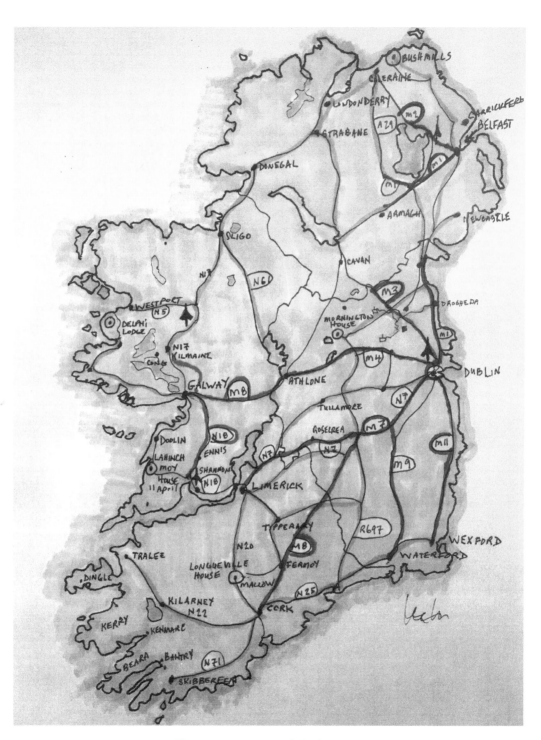

DRIVING MAP 11 APRIL

CHAPTER III

ON THE ROAD

I THOUGHT ABOUT WHAT HOME means to me, the home I personally know on the Great Lakes that I will take with me wherever I go, and of the home of my forebears now alien to me.

The Great Lakes influence all aspects of the culture and environment of those living within its watershed. In northern Michigan, a peninsula, we at the forty-fifth parallel of latitude live in the temperate zone where it's hot in summer, and snowy and cold in winter with a long muddy spring and a brilliant autumn. The freshwater of home is sweet and crisp. Living on the west-facing shore the lake is sixty miles wide, the wind flows over my face, and the setting sun lays down an orange path on the water leading me through life. This soil built my body. I know our plants, animals, and songs. I know the scent. I know and respect the people who lived here before my European ancestors arrived a hundred and fifty years ago. This is what I have to offer when I travel. It's important to know who I am, and to offer that as a gift.

Even though I hoped to offer my most authentic self, I was afraid to be rejected as an outsider in Ireland. I was afraid to be caught in a no-man's land as an American, with all of our cultural baggage, longing to connect to my ancient homeland and people. I was excited to make this pilgrimage to the home of my mothers, and I was especially so to be with my sisters.

The time for our trip was drawing near. On the 30th of March I was scheduled to leave with my friends for the first week, and after they returned home, I was eager to meet Liz, Jenni, and Josie in Lahinch on the west coast of Ireland, at Moy House.

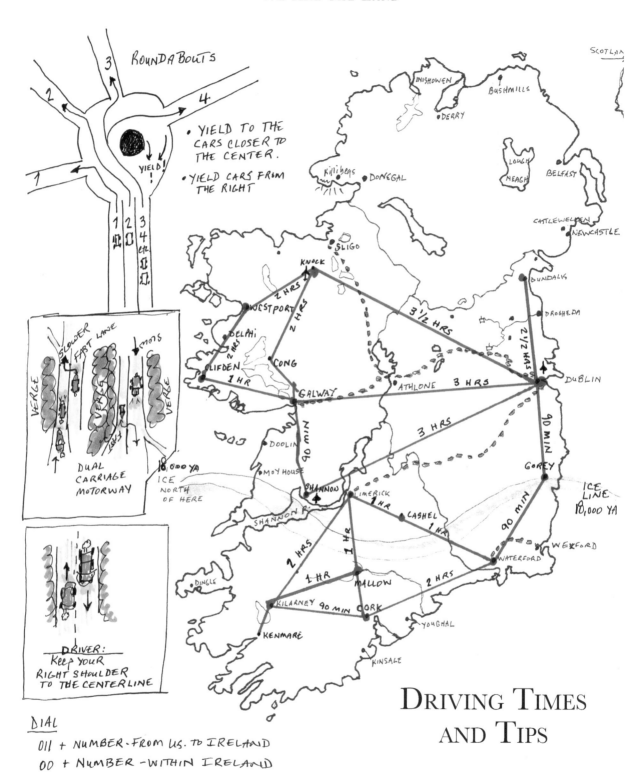

ROUNDABOUTS

- YIELD TO THE CARS CLOSER TO THE CENTER.
- YIELD CARS FROM THE RIGHT

YIELD!

SLOWER LANE
FAST LANE
SLOW
VERGE
VERGE
VERGE
DUAL CARRIAGE MOTORWAY

10,000 YA
ICE NORTH OF HERE

DRIVER: Keep your RIGHT SHOULDER TO THE CENTERLINE

SCOTLAND
INISHOWEN
BUSHMILLS
DERRY
LOUGH NEAGH
BELFAST
KILLIBEGS
DONEGAL
CATTLEWELLEN
NEWCASTLE
SLIGO
KNOCK
2 HRS
WESTPORT
3½ HRS
DUNDALK
DROGHEDA
DELPHI
2 HRS
2 HRS
2½ HRS
CLIFDEN
1 HR
CONG
GALWAY
ATHLONE
3 HRS
DUBLIN
DOOLIN
90 MIN
3 HRS
90 MIN
MOY HOUSE
GOREY
SHANNON
LIMERICK
1 HR
CASHEL
1 HR
ICE LINE
10,000 YA
SHANNON R.
2 HRS
1 HR
90 MIN
WATERFORD
WEXFORD
DINGLE
1 HR
MALLOW
2 HRS
KILARNEY
90 MIN
CORK
YOUGHAL
KENMARE
KINSALE

DRIVING TIMES AND TIPS

DIAL

011 + NUMBER - FROM US. TO IRELAND

00 + NUMBER - WITHIN IRELAND

As I planned the trip with my friends and family, I asked them what interested them most. Music and scenery was what they wanted. So I planned to drop us into the west coast with its rugged coastline and surf near the unofficial capitol of traditional Irish music in Doolin.

Wednesday 11 April
Moy House
Lahinch, Co. Clare

I knew yesterday morning I was sick after helping my friends board transportation to the Shannon Airport in Ireland. Most of us were feeling queasy this morning. Alone in my van, I left quickly for Moy House in Lahinch on the west coast with directions written on a small paper explaining the tricky roundabouts. I was worried about driving for two hours without stopping. And I wondered if I would find a bathroom if I did stop. I hurried on.

I was now at the lovely Moy House, but very sick with food poisoning. When I arrived at the beautiful, yet homey Moy House, the kind manager pointed out its features as we walked. I explained that I'd need to be in my room soon because I was quite ill. He showed me to the room and as he pointed out the drapes, and thermostat and such, I pointed out that I needed some time to freshen up RIGHT AWAY. At last he stepped out. I dashed into the bathroom only to stumble upon a crouching laborer painstakingly grouting a tile in front of the toilet into the floor.

Ohhh, no.

"Excuse me sir, could you finish that up at a later time?"

"No, lady, the tile covers a large hole in the floor that opens to the original well for the house," he said. "Look down in there. You can see it." He pointed. "You'll have to wait an hour before stepping on it."

Sweat popped out on my forehead as I sank into a chair near the door.

"I promise I won't step on it," I whispered.

At last he left. I didn't emerge from the bedroom for twenty-four hours mostly sleeping, fever raging, between frequent visits to the toilet. I was only

grateful that I'd not been lost enroute between the castle and the west coast. I later learned not all of my friends who flew home were as ill as I was on their flight, only those who had imbibed cocktails. The dedicated wine drinkers were fine. It must have been the ice.

Thursday 12 April
Moy House

I awoke at four in the morning. I flicked on the television. Men in a game ran kicking a ball, oh, soccer. But no, they caught the ball, and ran…was this rugby? No, running men tackled other men. Was I hallucinating? Sleep took me over. I later learned the game was called Gaelic and is a faster version of the others.

The next morning I woke weak, but without a fever to a fine day. This room at Moy House was lovely. The bed was in the part of the bedroom near the door to the hall with a wall separating the sleeping area from the sitting room on the other side. Daylight bathed this area through the glass walls and doors and snuck around the ends of the walls to the bedroom. I padded around to the sitting room. Stunned by the panorama of a large grassy, pebbled field sloping to the ocean, I stood transfixed at the door. Pulling it open, the scent of loam and salt water washed over me. My toes stuck out into the air across the sill. Beautiful horses grazed on the neighboring field. Oh my God, I loved this place. The solid whitewashed house with nine bedrooms, cozy entryway, comfortable dining room and tiled hallways felt like a home, not an inn. It was elegant, yet emotionally accessible.

Dressed, but barely recovered I decided to skip solid food. I sat on the front step in the sun with a cup of coffee waiting for my three sisters. Their plane was delayed until noon. Finally, with the sound of crunching gravel the transport pulled in, the door slid back, and they bounded out of the van.

"Hurray, we're here!" Hugs all around.

"Where are we?"

They milled about pulling bags from the van, sorting them in piles, looking up at the trees, peering at the back of the house.

"Your suitcase is on the left under the blue one where I put it," said Jenni.

We all know Jenni thinks she's the best at packing. At home, if Jen puts the spoons in a particular drawer, as we all do, she'll tell you to put your spoons in the same drawer at your house, too. She thinks she has figured out the ultimate best way to put away spoons. She's very helpful that way. And she'll come up with a marketing plan so the rest of the world won't be deprived of the best way to store spoons.

"Oh, my god, I can't believe we're finally here!"

"Yippee, we're in Ireland!"

"Just leave everything here," I said. "They'll bring it in. Let's go see the house and I'll show you around. But I have to warn you, I've been sick with food poisoning and am just starting to feel well enough to move."

The van pulled away as we headed into the house.

"Which is my room?"

After a little back and forth, Josie and Liz took one room to share, and Jen the third. They settled in. We peered out the windows at the grand sweep of lawn to the rocky, frothing shore and ocean beyond, and imagined curling up at the window with a book and the fire glowing. We were escorted around the house for a tour, oohing and ahhing at every charming object and delighting in the sitting rooms.

"Let's go to the cliffs of Moher!" They chimed in unison.

Would my energy hold out? Would I find a bathroom when I needed it? I made a last minute trip to the loo before climbing behind the wheel of our minivan. The cliffs of Moher, twenty minutes from Moy House, are some of the highest, steepest cliffs in all of Ireland, and one of the most popular and touristic attractions on the entire west coast. Maybe my sisters read about it on the airplane. It's one of those places you send a tourist if you know nothing about them, and they know nothing of Ireland. Giant motor coaches of tourists crowded the parking lot across the road from the cliffs. I was not at my best, but lagged behind keeping an eye out for the closest restrooms at the remarkable visitor center. Perhaps taking a cue from megalithic structures, the rock-faced visitor center was tucked behind a curving wall built into a huge hill. My sisters ran ahead to the simple rail that prevents the unwary from plunging into the sea past a three hundred and ninety

foot wall of banded rock with all the churning surf of this side of the Atlantic Ocean at its base. Next stop, oblivion.

I looked at them as they gazed over the cliffs, hair flying back. Jenni coltishly pranced up and down the fence line wanting to see everything, but not wanting to leave us behind. A castle tower of the O'Briens perched on a promontory above us to the north. We headed that direction. At the base of the tower I saw Liz turning slowly, looking at the ground, then looking out to sea.

She told me later, "It was magic. I felt like I was home. Deeply connected. There are lots of beautiful places I've been in the world, but not like that, not like I'd been there before."

Priding myself on driving as I do, I hate to admit when I make a mistake. I was driving on the left, in a big minivan, in a crowded parking lot, okay? The lane was marked EXIT. The payment booth was right there, but when I pulled in I was on the wrong side to pay up. *Damn.*

Josie, navigating, lowered the window, "Here you are, six euro."

The Irish never let a terrific moment of conversation slide. Our ticket lady leaned into the window toward me and said with a smile, "Well, I've just had my first bitch of the day!"

Shocked at her language, I must have blushed, "Yeah, sorry! I'm going backwards."

"No worries," she said, "Happens all the time, just remember while driving in Ireland, keep the bitch in the ditch!"

That I will not forget as the driver. Right shoulder to the centerline, and keep the…you know.

Next stop, the Cornerstone Pub so Josie could have her first Guinness in Ireland. She had pledged to have one a day. And so she did. It tasted of cinnamon and toasted barley. The thick creamy head, straight from the tap, was topped with the tiny image of a shamrock in the froth. They say the second serving of Guinness tastes like angel's breath.

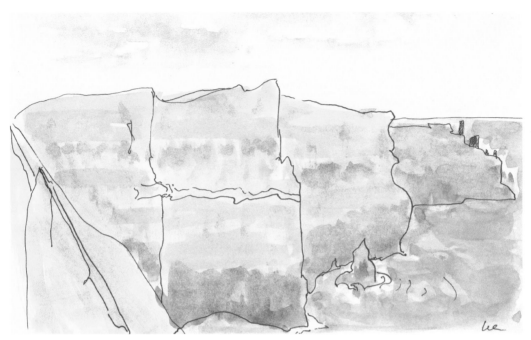

The Cliffs of Moher

Friday 13 April
Moy House

Off touring to Spanish Point in Milltown Malbay where we watched many surfers in the water at one of the best breaks in County Clare. Long rollers stacked up parallel to the shore carrying seal-like surfers to the mostly sandy bay. This wind in the face reminds me of home with my westerly facing house on Lake Michigan. The sun sets in the right place here, but the air is heavy with the deep mineral tang of seaweed and sea creatures unlike home where the freshwater air seems lighter, crisper, and smells of driftwood and pine. The crashing surf here has a long, low crescendo whereas the steep, deceptively dangerous waves at home pound the shoreline in staccato. By comparison, I wondered if my immigrating ancestors felt they were home when they reached the west facing shores of the great lake as I do? Different, and yet so profoundly right.

Josie, Jenni, Liz, Leslie

An interpretive sign related how part of the Spanish Armada sent by King Phillip II to invade England was wrecked here in 1588 in a terrible storm. Hundreds of Spaniards were drowned, and those who survived were hung and buried nearby.

This excursion called for a stop in Kilbaha at Keatings pub for Josie's daily Guinness, a bowl of marvelous Irish soup and bread, and a pit stop. We sat under the windows at a long table looking out over the strand and ocean and ordered from the menu. Soup in Ireland is thick and savory. In Michigan, it would be loaded with cream, but in Ireland the soup is simple, delicious and healthfully made of blended vegetables with herbs and meats added. The bread is thick, dark, and moist. To me, soup and bread is a full meal. To the Irish it's a snack. Many times at home after the trip, I thought how I'd love to have that soup again. What I wouldn't give to be there now.

At two, we drove out to remote Loop Head point on the ocean side of the Shannon River mouth. It's exhilarating to experience the danger that faces American tourists who expect handrails and safety precautions instead

of common sense and native caution. As not one inch of the cliff edge was protected we crept slowly to the precipice to stare three hundred feet down to the churning surf. Whoa, with a touch of vertigo, I hung back and leaned forward to draw.

As soon as I'm out from behind the wheel, my sketchbook is in my hand. The others might ooh and aah, snapping pictures and then say, "Okay, time to go!" I have to draw fast, because I don't know if I'll have thirty seconds, or five minutes. It's only when I'm seated at dinner or in a pub that I have time to draw more closely. While I enjoy drawing, it's mostly when I travel that I have time to do it. More than for the purpose of producing a picture, I draw when I travel because it helps me see. Drawing forces me to concentrate on the details, colors, the shadows, the sizes and shapes, and as importantly, movement. Then I'll remember it forever.

Loop Head was orginally named Leap Head after the legend of fleeing lovers Diarmid and Grainne leaping from the main peninsula to a towering stack just off the coast. Tales of young men lost on the beaches below the unprotected cliffs caught in the rising tide advise those visitors brave enough to descend to carefully consult their tide tables to avoid treading water that can quickly rise from under one foot to four feet of ocean at the base of the cliff. People from Michigan are accustomed to only six inch tides. In Ireland a fast tide and sheer cliffs are deadly.

We stopped in at Cooney's Tavern in the little town of Quilty with its intricate window detail so Josie could have a Guinness, aka Leslie can use the bathroom. And Josie could have another Guinness. While we waited to be served, I looked at locals at a neighboring table and was surprised to see my friend Judy's mother. Then I realized that it could not actually be her mother; it was someone who looked exactly like her. I later found out her mother's family had emigrated from a town up the coast from Quilty. By the end of the trip we all saw people we thought we knew at home. Intrigued by this woman's resemblance I almost spoke to her about her roots. But I'm not like Liz who will speak to any stranger, so we went on to Moor Bay.

By three p.m. we reached Kilkee at the Stella Maris (Star of the Sea) for a late lunch. No rock shop. Both Josie and I are interested in geology and wanted to take home souvenirs of local rocks. This town must be a hopping resort spot in sunnier July and August. Visitors to Ireland often try to avoid the famous rains in other seasons, but on this and future trips I had remarkably good luck in spring and autumn. Little cottages lined the strand on the cove, lots of shops sat on the square, and apartments stacked up overlooking the water.

A traumatic event for the local people occurred here in the mid 1800s. They were denied a place for Catholic worship by the English landlords. The local priest, Father Meehan, was not deterred and ordered construction of a box on wheels, an ark of sorts, the little ark of Kilbaha. To hold mass and baptisms, the local Catholics pulled the ark into and across the strand, the land uncovered by the receding tide. This land was owned by no man. By 1853, the faithful met at the ark for mass, baptisms, and last sacraments for five years before being granted a proper site for a church.

13 April 07

At Cooney's Tavern in Quilty so "Josie can have a guinness" aka Leslie can use the bathroom.

At Cooney's Tavern in Quilty

3pm – In Killkee at the Stella Maris for a late lunch. This town must be the hopping resort spot in season. Little cottages line the strand on the cove, lots of shops on the square, apartments stacked up.

6pm Lahinch
Stopped for a drink and light supper here at the Atlantic Hotel while we discuss our route for tomorrow.

Oh, I have lots of change, dear

Overheard at the Atlantic Hotel

Overheard at the Atlantic Hotel, "Oh, I have lots of change, dear."
Excerpted from my travel journal.

An abandoned estate.

CHAPTER IV

JUST ENOUGH EARLY HISTORY OF IRELAND

We recreate the offspring of our hearts and minds,
see for ourselves the boundaries of wilderness,
explore the edges of immensity in skies
so dark that sacks of billowing starlight unfurl
to spill them out across an undulating lake.

~Leslie Lee, *Sacred Space*

BY THE TIME I LEFT HOME in Michigan for this trip, I tried to learn some of the basics of Irish history. We only have three hundred years of U.S. history to learn as opposed to ten thousand for the Irish. In my brief winter education I learned enough to be shocked.

Because of their adoption of early Christian practices beginning before AD 500, Ireland became known as "the land of saints and scholars." The Irish established monasteries for worship and education across Ireland in the sixth and seventh centuries. These served as sanctuaries of learning for visiting scholars and theologians from across the world as well. They became famous for their collections of manuscripts and development of libraries. However, raiding Vikings of the eighth and ninth centuries ransacked the monasteries for their treasures. This brought an end to the golden era of Christian learning in Ireland.

From AD 800 to AD 1000 Ireland suffered the depredations of the Vikings culminating in their ouster after they lost to the warriors of Brian Boru, High King of Ireland, at the Battle of Clontarf. Brian Boru was treacherously

killed. Ireland then endured nearly a thousand years of domination first by the Normans from France, and later still by the English. Each carved up territory or property for its own people in this fertile, productive land. The Normans imposed their feudal system on the prior Irish system of provincial and territorial Kings and High Kings, and successfully blended their population into the native Irish.

Unlike the Normans, when the English came between the fourteenth and seventeenth century, they carried out a thorough colonization designed to subjugate and destroy the local inhabitants. They began quietly as their surveyors reshaped districts, parishes, and dioceses, renamed towns and provinces. They then imposed the English language and followed by filling positions of authority with their own. They then forcibly confiscated the land for a relatively tiny ruling elite who wielded enormous power. Forests were cut to build ships and longbows. They followed with war.

In 1628 Oliver Cromwell came to power. Revered in England and reviled in Ireland, he continued land confiscations. His troops laid siege to Irish cities cruelly butchering inhabitants. Moving through the countryside they killed so many native Irish only a third of the former population remained when they finished. Cromwell forbade Catholic worship and imposed penal laws on the remaining locals. Even after his death the English confiscation of Ireland continued. They seized an additional eleven million acres of land for their own, closed schools, and banished the remaining Irish Catholics of the region to live west of the Shannon River on the poorest land. The Catholics in Ulster fared a similar fate. By 1703 only fourteen percent of Irish land was owned by the native Irish. From beginning to end, the Irish fought for their land, their people, and their beliefs holding on as best they could. It is incredible that so much destruction was caused not by a difference in religious belief, but rather as an excuse for stealing the bounty of Ireland to increase English power and wealth.

The next hundred years saw unrelieved devastation for the Irish. Laws against Catholics and the Irish woolen trade were enacted. Battles raged. While England turned its armies and fleets to put down the rebellion in the American colonies, the Irish pushed for reforms only to again suffer English domination through the remainder of the century.

The natural rock stack at the Cliffs of Moher looking to America.

RED HAIR... WHO'S YOUR DADDY?

The high incidence of red hair in Ireland and Scotland can be attributed not to the Vikings, but more to the earlier invasion of the Pontic Steppes people. These were the Celts, also called the Gaels. Four thousand years ago they arrived with the genetic variant MC1R, a trait originating in the region of Iran today. As a recessive genetic trait, both parents must carry this MC1R gene variant for one in four of their children to have red hair. Less than two percent of the world's population have red hair. That compares to ten percent of Ireland's population with red hair, and thirteen percent of Scotland's population.

Your red hair is from your daddy and your mommy.

In the Great Famine, the potato blight wiped out the major food source for the Irish in 1845. Many English landowners exacerbated Irish misery by forcibly evicting Irish tenants from their estates. Homeless of all ages, the native Irish suffered the elements of nature, disease, and death. By 1853, a quarter of a million Irish were permanently expelled from their small crofts on English-Irish estates. The ruthlessness of these clearances to rid English estates in Ireland of poor smallholders left a legacy of enduring hatred for the landed gentry of England, the richest country in the world. The English exported Irish wheat, butter, beef and lamb to themselves and their distant colonies during the famine. Two million native people of a population of eight million starved, died of disease, or immigrated by 1859.

It is hard for me to reconcile the cruel behavior of my mixed English, Scots, and Irish ancestry. Here at home in Michigan, I now live with the privileges of the ruling class in a nation of immigrants following the violent uprooting of the Native American population and usurpation of land in America by the English, Scots, and Irish, and the rest. Our U.S. history included the atrocious practice of human slavery. My personal religious practice asks forgiveness for my forebears, and prayers that I will treat others as I myself wish to be treated.

Friday 13 April
Moy House
Lahinch, County Clare

Six in the evening in Lahinch. We stopped for a drink and light supper at the Atlantic Hotel while we discussed our route for tomorrow to Longueville House in Mallow.

Driving the coast road back to Moy House we passed various cottage enterprises including wild pitch golf courses tucked into tall grasses along the dunes, and a billboard proclaiming, "Pony trekking, Try it, you'll like it!"

Jenni said, "Oh! Maybe we can do that before we leave Ireland. I'd love that!"

"Jenni, we don't have time now," I said. "But maybe on the way back when we're here again before flying home."

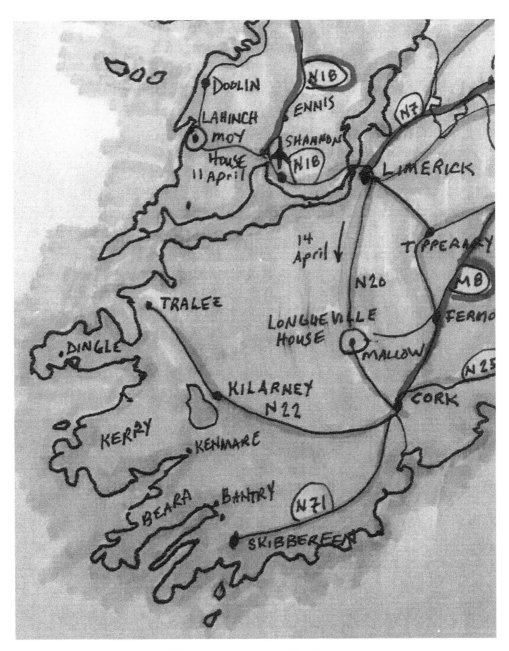

DRIVING MAP 13 APRIL

The front door of gracious Longueville House.

CHAPTER V

COUNTY CORK

A white oak tree beside the creek, roots deep in soil,
then pillars up, with mirrored branches arching out
to bind the shadows of the Earth to heaven's sun.
It lives along a row of comrades cut for life,
their spirits born anew by human will to build.

~Leslie Lee, *Sacred Space*

Saturday 14 April
Longueville House
Mallow, Co. Cork

SOMEHOW SIMPLY DRIVING in the Blackwater River valley is lovely. Gently sloping pale green hills bend toward the curving river. Longueville House rests graciously on a rise above its long driveway. At the pale blue door we parked to unload. The wonderful old family home of the O'Callaghans welcomed us. Tea at 3:45 p.m. We stood chatting at the door amid our growing mountain of bags when Jenni spied a hobby horse on a stick in the umbrella stand.

"Look what I found, do you remember these? We all had them," she said.

Out came the hobby horse. Jenni jumped on and galloped up and down the drive. Josie and I made little neighing sounds for her.

Turning to gaze down the huge slope of lawn, we marveled at the enormous old oaks in the field below. These oaks, we later learned, were plant-ed in honor of the 1815 battle formation of Wellington's troops at Waterloo to

celebrate their victory. Later still, we learned this O'Callaghan family was deprived of their property by Cromwell's troops in 1650. The land was returned to the family in 1938. Learning that about this very place made history come alive for me. The early 1900s was the setting for much debate on land reform in Ireland as the country struggled for independence and restitution.

Southwest Cork and the Blackwater River Valley

~Southwest Cork~

• Handdrawn by Leslie Lee - Not to Scale from Homann's Map of 1712.
• Names from Edward MacLysaght, The Surnames of Ireland.

Tonight we'll dine in the more formal conservatory. But first, after toting bags to our rooms, we wanted to explore the territory of the valley. As I walked down the hall to my room, I paused to look closely at an old black and white photograph at the head of the stairs. It was a group shot. In it was a woman, the image of my grandmother, Dorothy Waite, my mother's mother. But of course, it could not be as she never was in Ireland.

At home, before our departure for Ireland, I discovered Boherbue in the Barony of Duhallow, County Cork, Ireland. Liz had called with news of a discovery.

"Oh, my gosh, during my family searches, I found the names Patrick Quinlan and Ellen Dineen. They sailed on a ship in 1849. They may be our emigrating Quinlans."

I went into action. Okay, I asked myself, what was a Barony? Research revealed it was a subdivision of land imposed during the Tudor conquest. What did Boherbue mean? *The yellow road.* I imagined these distant relatives in romantic sounding Duhallow, *the land of the Munster Blackwater River.* The Kingdom of Munster was the southernmost of four provinces of Ireland. From my west facing home in northern Michigan I traced the roads and rivers of this area on my ancient map of Ireland.

I think many people who live in the *land of their people,* who haven't moved away from their homeland, wherever that is, can't understand the deep longing of those of us who have been severed from our lineages and groundings. It's akin to seeking one's long lost mother, a loving mother who by no fault of her own has lost track of her offspring. Does the motherland weep as a part of her sails away? Will there always be the magnetic draw tugging at the heart? It must be difficult for the Irish who remained in Ireland to have so many Americans and Australians trying to reconnect their severed personal histories. The people of Ireland are welcoming and kind, but I don't believe they think of us as Irish anymore. Perhaps, *of Ireland* is more accurate.

Here we were, at last, actually in Duhallow. The terrain rolled and rose in emerald waves, leaves on the trees were beginning to burst out in tiny green beginnings, mist dipped and rose over distant ridges. On we drove envisioning our distant ancestors alive in this place, raising their

children, and working the land over thousands of years. In two days we were to meet Father Kineely, at the Presbytery of St. Mary's parish to search their records.

On our way through the town of Millstreet we stopped in a bookstore. The proprietress there asked if we were Americans searching for our families, as so many do.

"Yes, we are. We're from Michigan, and we're here to try to find our father's line and our mother's line. Our story is that our mother's people were from County Cork."

" What is the name of your mother's Irish relative?" she asked.

We piped, "We know our great-great-great-grandfather on our mother's line came in 1849 was named Patrick Quinlan, and on a shipping manifest we found a Patrick Quinlan traveling with Ellen Dineen. They're listed in the parish records at Duhallow where we're headed to look into it."

We stood among the shelves of books.

She studied each of us carefully in the face, pursed her dubious lips, shook her head, and said, "Hmmm, Dineen? I don't think so."

What was it she had seen? I was mystified and a bit disappointed she read in our faces that we were not part of the Dineen clan.

"Well, do we look Irish anyway?" Jenni asked.

She looked at Jenni, "You don't," then looked at Liz, "Or you," looked at Josie carefully, "Or you." She looked at me, "But you do."

Undaunted, we four middle-aged sisters piled back in the van to continue to explore the land and ancestry of our forebears. At last, we turned into the town, so long a dot with a highlighter halo on my map of Ireland, and slowly cruised the streets of Boherbue marveling at the colorful houses and quaint byways. We were on the sharp lookout for the St. Mary's parish church in Mill Sreet where our potential forebears were baptized. We found it across from Murphy's pub.

"It's time for a Guinness!" Josie declared.

"And I for a Cork gin!" I chimed.

Wondering if it might be bad form, I nevertheless took a prominent parking spot in the empty church lot before crossing to the pub. In deference to

the parish, we read grave markers before turning toward Murphy's. We chatted with the locals once inside. The Irish are the most hospitable people I've ever met, ready with food and drink, music, and scintillating wit. They prize good conversation, called *the craic*, and a tale well told. At pubs and parties it is customary for people to share a bit of themselves by performing their favorite song, poem, or dance. Liz, the most outgoing, approached a couple who sat at the bar to ask if they knew of the church and who might have records. This kind man took Liz outside, knocked on some doors and offered to take us down to the presbytery. But it was nearly time for our dinner reservation.

"No, thanks, we have to go soon, but we'll be back." she said.

The kind man looked at her and asked, "Now, which one of you ladies will be driving?"

Liz pointed to me and said, "My sister, Leslie, is the driver."

"Oh, the one in the pub with the gin?" he smiled sweetly and asked.

I blushed. Time to go. I learned the limit for drinking and driving in Ireland was not one, but zero. Walking a very straight line to the church parking lot, we continued on around to the front where more gravestones poked out of the ground on the old side of the cemetery. Thinking to look at markers I stepped out on the spongy grass, but as my foot sank in a bit I paused in horror at the thought of sinking into someone's grave.

With a little shiver and rising stomach contents, "Euuuu! What is thaat? Time to get out of here!"

We Americans aren't accustomed to real, old stuff. Shaken, we clambered into the van, I put the car in gear, then turned the wrong direction heading out of town. It was an otherwise lovely, narrow, undulating, winding road bordered by rock walls on one side and hedgerow on the other typical of the region. We drove a few kilometers without seeing another house or even a passing car before I found a turnaround spot.

I pulled in thinking about which lane I would be backing into, and repeated the mantra as I reversed, "Stay on the left, shoulder to the centerline, bitch in the ditch."

Out on the road, on the left, such as it is when the road is too narrow to have two lanes, Jenni called out, "Wait! I have to pee."

I stopped the car and put it in park. Jenni jumped out the sliding door, looked around for a place with privacy, but found nothing but walls bounding both sides.

"Okay you guys, I'm just gonna go in the road behind the car. Don't leave me!"

She dropped her pants right in the middle of the lane. From the rear-view mirror, so far so good, no car was visible from behind. My eyes flicked forward. *Uh-oh.* Just coming over the rise the front of a car was cresting the hill. I realized they wouldn't have enough room to get by us unless I pulled off to the left. With my foot on the brake, I put the car in gear to inch it up and to the left a little. Jenni's head snapped up, and before I could stop again, she panicked and began running with her legs spread apart to keep her pants from falling off. There she was in the rear-view mirror jolting down the road with her pants stretched between her feet penguin-style. The other car slowly approached.

"Hey, wait! You guys, wait!"

I think she didn't see the oncoming car and thought I was playing the joke on her that she would have played on me. The car moved over, but it was still too close. Just as Jenni got to our car, I had to move up again. My foot came off the brake to squeeze over.

"Waaiiiit!"

To inch up, I drove a little farther forward and to the left until our car brushed against the hedge. It was at that point I think Jenni saw the oncoming car and galloping with all her might, she reached us and dropped down behind the van to hide. The other car drove slowly past and off down the road at a steady pace. I hope they had as good a laugh as we had.

Jenni, pants pulled up, flung the door open, and asked, "Does anyone have an extra pair of pants?"

Miraculously, I had. Changed and dry with Jenni calmed down and ready for the drive, we set off in the right direction for Longueville House. Among us as a team, I was the amateur historian, and driver; Josie, the navigator and gastronome; Liz, the genealogist and unofficial photographer and Jenni, well, Jenni didn't have a well-defined task other than to read the *Blue Guide* to us. That was until this day, Saturday, the 14th of April.

Josie and Jenni

Chapter VI

Return of the Bull

Twenty Minutes Later, tooling back through the valley, I was driving on the left, of course, right shoulder to the centerline, on the highway at eighty kilometers per hour with three lanes of cars returning home at the end of the day. Gentrified farms blurred on our left, a hedgerow separated opposing traffic that flew past on my right shoulder when, suddenly the tail lights of distant cars flared red. I looked ahead to my right, and pressed against the hedge in the narrow median was a cowering baby brown cow, a calf. I braked hard. I flicked on emergency lights and other cars began to slow. The calf turned to run into the traffic.

Jenni shouted, "Cow!"

I fully stopped. Other cars around us slowed, pulled over, or froze in their lane.

I yelled, "Go get him Jenni!"

Jenni flung open the sliding door and leapt into the highway. I glanced to my left. Twelve feet high gates on the side of the road read, *Blackwater Stud Farm*. This beautiful, and valuable, new brown calf had somehow escaped its pasture, trotted through the iron entry gates, across traffic, and now cowered against the greenery in the middle of the highway. I was afraid he would break through the hedge directly in front of the invisible speeding oncoming cars.

"Herd him, Jenni, but don't scare him!"

" Josie, go, go! One person can't herd a cow!"

Out jumped Josie amongst the cars. Sure enough, Jenni, in true cowgirl fashion, had cut away the calf from the hedge and had him moving away from the unseen traffic toward the gates. Josie stood in front of the rows of cars, arms

out, so he wouldn't come her way. Between the cars, through the gauntlet of Jenni and Josie, into the gates, the little calf ran. As soon as the calf cleared the entrance, I parked our car off the roadway in front of them, slipped inside, and closed the two tall stud farm gates behind me so he couldn't go out. Josie moved inside and disguised herself behind a farm gate so as not to scare him.

MOOOOO!

Deep bellowing rose from a huge animal inside a pasture enclosure next to us. Our heads swiveled to stare at the beast. At first I thought it was a bull, but no, it was a she. This mother was enormous. Masses of muscles and bone rippled under loose dark dun-colored hide as she moved along the far fence line bellowing for her calf. The calf, a baby bull, four and a half feet tall, and at least six hundred pounds, was the same beautiful soft brown.

Mooooo! Moooo!

He tried to squeeze his little body through the rails. With his head he rammed the gate of the pen. Bang! He rammed it again. Bang! A chain looped through the rails. Josie searched for a lock and tugged on the pasture gate but it would not open. Perhaps that was best. I imagined the massive upset mother cow bursting out, trampling us, or tossing us around like so much fluff.

MOOOOOO!

Thwarted, the baby bull turned suddenly and trotted up the driveway toward the main house.

"Go, Jenni. Go!"

One might wonder why Jenni was the herder, but we three knew she always wanted to be a cowgirl, and had even gone on a roundup at a cow herding camp.

Lovely horses in other enclosures attended to these proceedings with keen, intelligent interest, and concern. Their heads turned in unison to watch the activity of our hero, Jenni, and the little brown cow. The calf headed up the rising, curving driveway. Jenni jogged after him. The calf ran into bushes at the entrance. While he thought he was hidden, Jenni ran up the steps to the door of the manor house and banged the knocker. She sneaked around a hedge to outsmart the little cow.

A loud *MAAOOOOO* rose from the mother down below.

Out of the bushes burst the baby calf. He trotted down the drive back toward his mother's enclosure. I held out my arms as he approached trying to look large enough to block the path opposite her gate. Josie was still at the pasture gate, and Liz stood near the tall, iron front gates, hands clasped in front of herself, poised to run away if the calf came her way.

He stopped and looked at me, I called sweetly, "Come, boss." He stepped forward, hopefully, then suspecting trickery shied toward Josie, then bolted from her, perhaps remembering the head-banging gate, and ran directly at Liz.

"What am Ieeeee supposed to…?" Agghhhh!" she wailed and dodged.

The calf cut to the right of Liz and disappeared along the fence line of the now closed entrance gates. Jenni, panting, trotted down the drive.

Oh, no! Was there a break in the fence on the highway? We sisters had presented a perfect U shape that had forced the little cow away. Would he pop out onto the highway into traffic? Oh no! No, the top of his head reappeared inside the pen. He raced straight to his mother, tucked under and began nursing. Somehow, he had slipped through a hidden, narrow space between the fence posts, the same from which he must have escaped. At last all was well.

In pulled a blue truck with two neighbors from the next farm over. We let them in. They heard about the calf on the highway, and told us they would inform the owners who were away. Whew! We piled back in the van and out on the road, I, the driver, Liz the genealogist, Josie the navigator, and, Jenni, the herder of the studly brown cow of the Blackwater valley. Jenni had a job.

I asked as we drove along, "Hey, Jenni, did I ever tell you Ireland's most well-known legend, the Tain Bo Cuailgne? About the brown bull of Cooley, and how he was stolen, returned, and the war he caused?"

And as I asked her, I thought of the story I might tell tonight at dinner about the four middle-aged Irish-American ladies who themselves returned a little bull in Ireland.

Longueville House
Still 14 April

Tonight we dined in the conservatory at Longueville House—Josie on duck paté and duck confit, Jenni on wild sea bass with saffron risotto and prawn consommé, Leslie, ditto, Liz on provencal vegetables with lamb loin and Irish beef. We reveled in the adventures of the day.

"Jenni's Words of the Day," non-sequitors, were both puzzling and hilarious, and became a staple of our fun times together. We had waited a long time after our entrees for the tart tartin and cheese and other beautiful desserts. Finally, they arrived.

And in Jenni's special way she exclaimed, "Hey, that's why it took so long, they had to make all this!"

Josie and Jenni at dinner in the conservatory.

15ᵗ April 2007

Glouthane Standing Stone

CHAPTER VII

THE SEARCH FOR OUR IRISH MOTHER

Within the secret chambers of the house, we light
the flame we carry with us to humanity,
then find the rock on which to stand to orient
ourselves within opposing forces of our peers,
and only then, we may unite the outer world.

~Leslie Lee, *Sacred Space*

Tuesday 15 April
Longueville House

THIS DAY WE DROVE LONG around the beautiful mountainous Beara Peninsula in West Cork. Each of the four southwesterly pointing peninsulas of Ireland is spectacular. Just beyond the town of Millstreet we stopped to look over the Glouthane standing stones, thought to be ancient boundary markers. As I was quietly drawing the stones, Black Angus cows in the nearby field became curious about me. One by one they slowly walked to the fence until there was a crowd gazing at me with their hopeful, curious brown eyes. I continued drawing. Josie came up beside me laughing to tell me that it looked as though I was reading a fascinating story to a herd of cows. We continued on to Glengarriff where we ate lunch looking out over beautiful Bantry Bay with an array of large boats anchored out in the harbor.

I love these exhilarating roads across the bases of the peninsulas.

Glouthane Standing Stone

West outside of Mill street

They roll from the ocean up over the mountains and down to the next, like tracing across the knuckles of your hand with fingers spread.

Back at Longueville House we met Liz's diplomatic friends, Andrew and Kathy for drinks and dinner.

Jenni's Words of the Day:

"Why does the champagne go to your head?" she wondered. "Oh, because the bubbles go up!" she declared.

Monday 16 April
Longueville House

A walk began the day, followed by a delicious buffet breakfast in the morning room. We met Jane O'Callaghan, owner of Longueville House, who gave us detailed travel information.

When Jenni helped herself to the yogurt, Jane scooped up granola unbidden sprinkling it on top of Jenni's food, saying, "It'll be good for you!"

Andrew called it the Callaghan treatment.

We spent the day in Killarney, first, to Mallow to the Heritage Center where we struck out. We were disappointed to learn the parish records of St. Mary's were part of County Kerry, not County Cork. We continued our search in Killarney in a small library collection for more research. It was a beautiful though not terribly productive day.

The jacket of the winning race dog, Ladbroke,
framed on the wall of the Speakeasy Pub in Killarney.

Tuesday 17 April
Longueville House

At last we met Father James Kineely. He was extremely handsome and had our full attention. Louis and Ann McCarthy helped us research their 1835 parish records. In the small office we sat on chairs, our knees almost touching, as Father Kineely pulled old books out to page through.

He found Patrick Quinlan and Ellen Dineen. Reading the tiny script, he looked up and said, "I don't think this is your relative."

"Oh?" We each peered at the book and passed it on. I couldn't read the tiny old script well.

Father Kineely explained the phrase *unnatural child* or something like that. Perhaps meaning out of wedlock, or another term we didn't understand. Disappointed, but grateful for the help, we thanked them and left.

It's a strange phenomenon to emotionally attach oneself to a name and place as I had, as if mystical filaments float out of the ground to the soul longing for connection. Sadly, I detached myself from these invisible threads, rolled up the yellow road in my mind, and said goodbye to beautiful Duhallow. I closed the dictionary written by Father Dineen. We knew our great-great-great-grandfather was Patrick Quinlan, but who was his wife?

It just isn't fair that our cultural mind-set is to identify solely and intensely with our paternal name, our last name, as if that one line explains our ancestry. Men certainly feel the direct male line connection more strongly than any other genetic or ancestral input. Consider the Junior, Senior, I, II, III add-ons. However, each person's direct genetic ancestry consists of two equal lines, maternal and paternal, multiplied by four for each successive generation. We unfortunately don't know much about our maternal lines, because a wife's maiden name, and her mother's often weren't recorded. Many Americans don't know the maiden names of their grandmothers. And even if they did, that name was paternal and again changed with marriage. These feelings of pride, identity, and belonging that we have for our father's name have been lost on the maternal side. Until now.

Genetic tests tell us something more about our maternal ancestors

from the beginning of time, just not with a surname. To help others understand these women of thirty-five thousand years ago were real, living, breathing ancestors, geneticist Bryan Sykes nicknamed the clan mother H, Helena. A name, not just a letter. It's hard to grasp that she was a real woman living in Europe somewhere. She bore daughters who also bore daughters, as direct as a paternal line, all successfully born and reared to my sisters and me. Along the way these H women peopled nearly half of the maternal ancestry of modern Europeans as well.

Years after our trip, Liz visited Catholic Riverside Cemetery in Kalamazoo, Michigan to discover our great-great-great-grandfather Patrick Quinlan and wife were buried there without markers. That set her on a trail to find information indicating our three times great-grandmother's name was Honora Irik, (anglicized to Herrick.) Both Honora and her daughter, Maggie, died in March of 1879 leaving behind a bereft husband, William Fisher, to raise his young daughter alone. He was a good and attentive father to little Nellie. Nellie was our great-grandmother. Perhaps we'll learn more information regarding the line of our ever-changing maternal names.

Recently, a perfect match on the computer to our maternal DNA revealed we are descended from a woman who lived in the last century named Bridget O'Donovan. She lived in the region of West Cork, near Skibbereen. Our search for our mother's Irish line would continue even while today's quest was ending.

It was too late to visit Cobh, the enormous harbor from which two and a half million Irish departed for America in the late 1800s, and the last port of call for the Titanic before sailing for America. Cork City, a university town, seems to the residents to be the true Irish capitol. We met Mr. O'Keefe in the library parking lot. We were on our way to the restaurant, Jacques, for dinner in Cork City. Josie had lamb tongue. Beautiful bridges arched over the River Lee that wound through the heart of the city several times.

In retrospect each of us, in our own way, were disappointed not to find our mother's line while we were in Ireland. I knew Liz would continue the search through genealogy and family records, while I continued down the path of genetic ancestry. Having touched the Irish land, we would not give up.

Jenni's Words of the Day:
"They always put gravel on their garden walks."

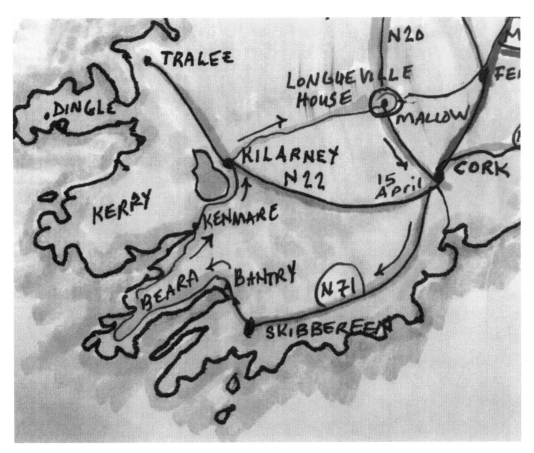

THE DRIVE AROUND THE BEARA PENINSULA 15 APRIL.

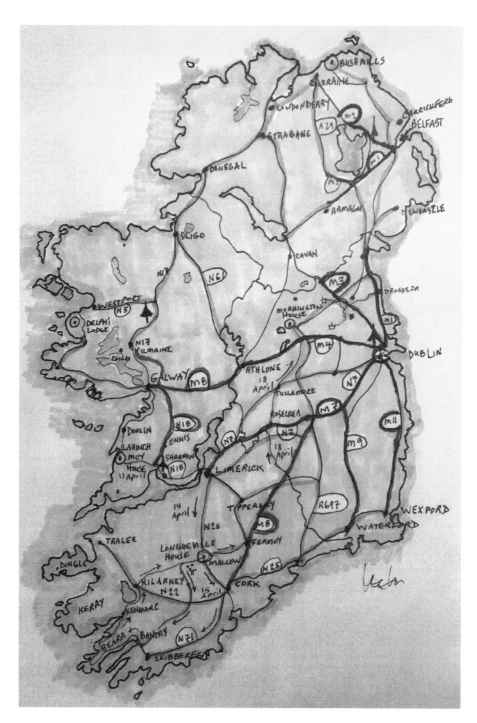

DRIVING MAP 18 APRIL

CHAPTER VIII

COUNTY WESTMEATH

Wednesday 18 April
From Longueville House, Mallow
To Mornington House
Multyfarnham, Co. Westmeath

AMID GOODBYES AND LUGGAGE packed into the van, this morning we departed the lovely Longueville House. We headed north enroute to Mornington House in County Westmeath where we hoped to visit the ancient megaliths of Newgrange, Knowth, and Dowth, and the early seat of the Kings of Ireland at the Hill of Tara. Liz, Jenni, and I were delighted to read that our family name, Quinlan, descends from the kingly line of the Southern UiNeill, one of whom was king in AD 432 when St. Patrick arrived to Christianize the people of Ireland. The Irish translation for Quinlan is O'Caoindealbhain.

On the road it was difficult to hear above the car noise and sisters chatting. I thought Liz said we were going to visit her friend from Guatemala, a Japanese Mayan.

"Your friend is a Japanese Mayan?" I asked when we stopped.

"No, my friend's name is Jacqueline Ryan," Liz answered.

It was an interesting visit nonetheless. We lunched at Morrisey's in Abbeyleix, after which we climbed the rocky outcrop at Dunamase, a National Monument of Ireland with a long history of fortification, pillaging, and habitation before the castle on top was destroyed.

As usual, we planned to dine at the house where we stayed on the first

night in new lodgings. After a long drive through the countryside I was exhausted and careful to stay off the roads after dark. Plus, I wanted a gin. And we needed to meet our new hosts Warwick and Ann O'Hara who settled us in after a long day on the road.

The house was large and set back across a gracious front lawn. It was equipped with an elevator to accommodate Ann who is wheelchair-bound. The house felt dark and gloomy with heavy window coverings in the public rooms. In fact, the house may have been so old it wasn't equipped with many electric lights. My room was lovely with large windows, and loaded with what appeared to be the original furniture from several hundred years ago. After I put my suitcase on the bed, Warwick explained with a grimace the lace covering the bed was from his grandmother. *Oops.*

Josie told me when I was working on the book she had only a cot in what she took to be the former servants' quarters. The rest of us never heard about it or saw it, and she didn't spend much time there. Warwick seemed to do everything and be everywhere, climbing off the tractor, showing us our rooms, with an apron on in the kitchen, or walking us down to Loch Derravaragh through the ash tree plantation.

"These trees are almost ready to be harvested even though they're only six inches in diameter," he explained. "Notice the bend at the bottom of each tree. We're growing them to become cricket bats, or hurling sticks."

Loch Derravaragh at Mornington House in County Westmeath.

Walking single file through the strange ash wood, the conversation about the lake, pastures, and the area passed up and down the line of us like a game of telephone.

By the time we reached the clearing at the edge of the lake Jenni turned to me and asked, "Do the sheep here eat bats?"

Before Warwick returned to the house to prepare dinner with Ann, he walked us out of the woods to the edge of the loch and told us the legend of the *Children of Lir*. The children were turned into various animals by a jealous stepmother and cursed to live three lifetimes in three different places in Ireland before they became people again. It was on this pretty loch the children were

Liz and Ann looking over the map of Wales.
Mornington House — 20 April 2007

Ann and Liz looking over the map of Wales.

doomed to live as swans. It is said this legend is the basis of the ballet Swan Lake.

For dinner we feasted on smoked salmon, sliced cucumbers in oil, walnut bread, herbed blini, carrot and orange soup puree, chicken boned with wing, herbs, tomatoes and garlic in juices, new potato, sea kale, spinach balls, salad lettuces, and for desert, a ball of chocolate mousse, a meringue Oreo, and sliced strawberries. The table was beautifully set with large candelabras perched effectively on either end rather than in the center so we could see each other well in the otherwise unlit dining room.

Ann explained details about the region we were to visit the next day. I've never met anyone as determined as Ann to look on the dark side of life and to comment on it. By the time we were off to bed on the first night, Ann told us about her dead best friend, lamenting she couldn't go to the funeral. She recalled she couldn't get between chairs in her wheel chair and that she had to go to England to buy her boat-sized shoes. She said not to let this old lady (her) bore you, she's a miracle worker but can't do everything anymore. She said she worked full time in a different position, and yet she had to reorganize the catering function at the school.

A typical charming Irish village.

Chapter IX

The Boyne Valley Megaliths

My memories are home in humble silence here
as scents of sea arise from limestone walls on days
of rain like this. I still can smell crustaceous salt
and pause in reverie as images of life
remind me of ancestral versions of myself.

~Leslie Lee, *Sacred Space*

Thursday 19 April
Mornington House

WE HAD AN EXTRAORDINARY FULL DAY touring Newgrange, Knowth, Dowth, the Hill of Tara, and Trim Castle.

How I loved driving through the old towns peppered along the twisty, narrow, rock-walled roads of Ireland. The multilane motorways built in the last twenty years had not yet turned the charming, authentic villages they passed into ghost towns. I hope they never lose the genuine charm of individual villages connected to each other by the old roads and the old ways. One still feels the rich street culture of pubs, music stores, and residences on the main streets. Flashes of brightly painted shops and houses cheer visitors. Sidewalks only wide enough for one person at a time line many streets. The men step into the gutter to allow women and children to pass. The outskirts of town sprout poles bristling with arrowed signs pointing to surrounding nearby villages. Often a rock post, pocked by the ages, marks the intersection.

I don't know how a country the size of Indiana can seem so large and diverse. I suppose one way is that roads curve so much they quadruple the distances. These roads curl around soft hills, traverse up and down mountains, and loop around three thousand miles of rugged coastline. I'm completely charmed not to see straight lines on the landscape. This entire island was inhabited before the surveyors arrived. Instead, lichen-covered rock walls weave and cross each other up hillsides following property lines that bend around natural features and leap over rivers in ever diminishing hedgerows of gorse and hawthorn. From the air, the land looks like an old-fashioned quilt of emerald green velvet stitched with yellow furze covering a bed of down stuffed rolling hills.

In the middle of any little town at milking time a wooden gate might swing open into the street blocking all traffic for a few minutes as a collection of cows are herded across to the barn from the neighboring field of fresh grass. The farmer stands by tapping a stick to his, or her, tall rubber boots, corduroy pant legs stuffed in at the tops, wearing a long, wool, grimy sweater prized for its natural water repellency. Centuries of good breeding and feeding on rich limestone grasses have developed beautiful cows and horses in Ireland. These animals are prized around the world, and the horse fairs in which they are sold and traded are a cultural experience not to be missed.

North of Dublin by fifty miles lies the Boyne River Valley, in Irish, *Bru na Boinne*. It is rich in ancient history, megaliths of six thousand years before at Newgrange, Knowth, and Dowth; ring forts on hilltops of more than a thousand years of High Kings at Slane and Tara; round towers; high crosses of Celtic Christianity; evidence of repeated Viking raids a thousand years ago; and churches and castles of Norman and English occupations. One feels the Boyne River in all of this territory, the curvaceous land slopes down to the river, the great megaliths were built nearby, the legendary *salmon of knowledge* swam these waters, and kings were ferried across the water in ceremony to the hill of Tara.

Everywhere we've traveled, stories, legends, and myths occupy the Irish cultural landscape reaching back not hundreds of years, but thousands upon thousands. This deep, deep layering of culture, landscape, and mythology is

Even the cows in Ireland know to walk in the left lane.

unknown to most Americans until they visit old, unbroken civilizations such as is found here. It's incredible to grasp how newborn the Western-European-American mindset is by comparison. Imagine how people of the old country might be unaware how imbedded their knowledge and culture is within themselves. It's everywhere around them from early age in their landscape, buildings, songs and stories. Why would they think it was different for anyone else?

Non-natives in America, Australia, and other long-time displaced peoples are characterized by this cultural amnesia. We are separated from our ancestral story as unnaturally as a shadow is separated from its body. Many of us don't know the names of our great grandparents, especially the maiden names of the grandmothers, and don't know the places where the old families lived in the old country, a place where antecedents may have lived for thousands upon thousands of years. I think of all the lost information of trades and professions, of recipes, songs, and habits normally handed down from generation to generation. Still, talents may have passed to the offspring in genetic traits. Many of us know someone who found out late in life they shared the same profession as a long line of ancestors.

Even in an early nomadic hunter-gatherer era, bands of people hunting large game regrouped through the knowledge of places and stories carried in their oral history and mythology. All I heard from my family was, "We're English and Scotch-Irish," and a few stories of my grandparents.

My relatives were busy hiding their Irish ancestry out of shame at being at the bottom of the cultural heap in anglophile America. Maybe we wouldn't have been so in love with the English if we had known or remembered what our Irish and Scottish relatives had to endure at the hands of the English before arriving in America. Was that a survival mechanism of our near ancestors? As much as it broke their hearts and fueled their anger, they remained silent as one generation after another distanced themselves from their roots. Generation one: An Irish Catholic couple were driven out of Ireland by the English. Generation two: Their daughter married a Scots Presbyterian, whose family was driven first out of Scotland, then out of Ireland by the English. Generation three: Their granddaughter married an English Episcopal, then she was safely accepted by English society in America. Ours was the American story.

CHIEF IRISH FESTIVALS are celebrated on the quarter year on the day in the middle cycle of the sun. Bonfires are lit. Festivals begin on the eve.
- February 1: **Imbolg,** the goddess Brigid, daughter of Dagda and patron of poetry, crafts and healing. The Green Man is celebrated now.
- May 1: **Bealtine,** bright light (*Bel*) plus (*tine*) means fire and celebrates the open pasturing and crops. Bonfires are lit.
- August 1: **Lunasa,** honoring the god Lugh who is young, beautiful and athletic. All celebrate the bountiful harvest.
- November 1: **Samain,** when the tombs are opened to allow the spirits of the dead to emerge and mingle with the living. People dress in costume to fool the spirits. It is All Hallow's Eve.

IMPORTANT IRISH GODS AND GODDESSES OF HISTORY
- **Dagda.** He is a good god who kills his enemies with one end of his club and heals them with the other end. His cauldron is always full of food.
- **Morrigan.** She is a goddess of war and tribal mother who protects her people in battle as well as a prophet and raven, the symbol of death.
- **Lugh's Talents.** He is a god of arts, music, poetry, and storytelling. He is a harpist, sorcerer, champion in sports and a craftsman. He protects the harvest and provides a good time.

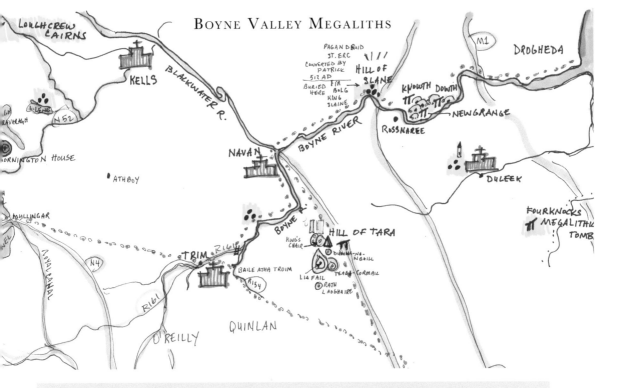

IN ANCIENT IRISH LAW, the Brehons were in a scholarly class. They specialized in interdisciplinary lore as an elite group of poets, druids, and judges. The king did not initiate the laws but was subject to them.

Honor price.

Every person had a value or honor price. If a crime was committed against that person, he or she was accordingly owed the price in goods or slaves. Poets had the highest honor price. If a person refused to grant hospitality or other serious offense, their honor price was reduced. All people had a social obligation to provide needed food and shelter for others. Even the king could not refuse those seeking help.

Compensation.

The Brehon determined one's value or honor price and the compensation to be paid in a legal dispute. For serious crimes, the next generation continued to pay the fine if necessary. However, if the perpetrator was proven ignorant of the law, the fine was cut in half. Unfair judgements were redressed. Laws governed accidents and injuries.

To build bonds of community and loyalty, children were fostered out of their families to others. Boys returned home at seventeen, girls at fourteen, the ages of marriage.

While satire for poets was prized, there were laws against mocking someone's appearance or giving a person an offensive nickname.

Women might be trained as poets or warriors. A wife owned what she brought with her to the marriage. Household work done by either partner was given credit. Divorce was allowed.

Slaves had rights. A pregnant slave was emancipated.

The entrance to Newgrange.

Chapter X

Newgrange

In Ireland, this enormous megalithic monument of ceremony and mystery is known as Bru na Boinne. It is an earthen dome thirty-six feet high and two hundred-forty feet across surrounded by ninety-seven engraved kerb stones. Most scholars call it a passage tomb. It is one of three known related structures situated on the banks of the Boyne River. At more than five thousand years old it is older than the pyramids, older than Stonehenge, and older than the tombs of Mycenae.

For years I've pursued an interest in ancient symbols. I've also been intrigued with the social and intellectual aspects of the people of the Mesolithic era of ten thousand to six thousand years ago, and Neolithic era of six thousand to four thousand years ago. I chose our lodgings at Mornington House to be close by, and called in advance for tickets to tour inside the ancient structures.

Because of my previous reading and study, I learned as much as possible about Newgrange. Yet as with all prehistory, even from the most reputable source, information is speculative. No one really knows why or how they were built and used by the inhabitants, or how the symbols relate to the activities that were taking place there. That certainly doesn't prevent experts from forming and stating their opinions, nor has it kept me from my own interpretations. So I was not a casual tourist, but a fairly well-informed and keenly interested person brimming with anticipation to see the symbols and the buildings first-hand. I was excited to be standing inside the very chambers of this profound antiquity.

We arrived early, got our badges and guide, and with our twenty fellow tourists rode the bus near to the huge mound where the dome of grass capped the brilliant white crescent, curving wall. Up the hill we labored until we stood

at the white quartz entry. Black stones unseen from a distance, had been spaced apart randomly across the entrance. The archeologists found them nearby and this is how they replaced them. The enormous, famous stone incised with swirls, diamond shapes, and lines laid across our path. I looked with interest at the boxy opening above the narrow portal to the interior.

The tour guide explained what we were seeing as we followed along into the darkness.

"This tunnel is twenty-four feet long, and here you have to bend down, now straighten up and turn sideways to pass through. Keep moving, everyone."

We crept along single file ducking and bending in various contortions to fit under and between the huge stones lining the tunnel. Strange symbolic swirls, diamond shapes and lines were carved in various places on the way in.

"Now we're in the chamber with its corbelled ceiling."

We each straightened up as we entered the round room. Everyone peered into the semi-darkness. Many symbols were carved into the stones in specific, but mysterious places. We stood packed elbow to elbow under the interior dome of interlaced rock.

The guide continued,"…and you'll notice the three small rooms, left, right and straight ahead with their stone basins. Human ashes and bone fragments have been found under and around these basins with these perfectly round, stone balls."

The hairs on my arms rose as I studied the symbols, basins, stone balls, and the placement of everything.

The guide continued. "Now, you, you and you stand over there, and you, you and you move to the right and clear this path down the tunnel. With my flashlight, I will simulate the sunbeam coming through the upper window above the portal on the only day of the year that it reaches this chamber, on the winter solstice. The light travels down the tunnel to illuminate these back chambers. Starting over here on the left chamber, the beam of light sweeps across the floor, through the domed room across to the central chamber, then over to this chamber on the right. Within seventeen minutes the beam of sunlight will have entered, traveled across the rooms, and completed its journey out the tunnel only to return at the same time and day next year."

Left Chamber

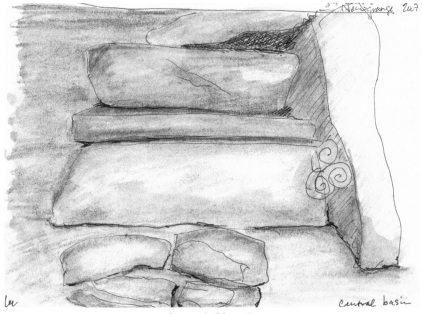

Central Chamber

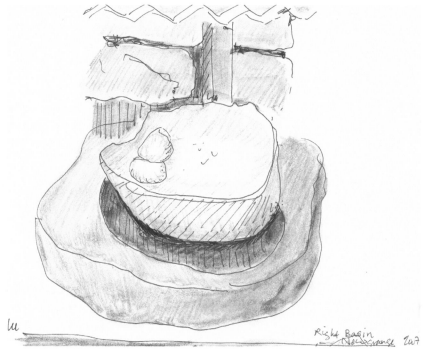

Right Chamber

I was starting to feel our group was transported to a parallel universe and were trapped in the next world together having shared the same bizarre experience.

Finally our guide said, "Okay, time to leave."

There was a collective sigh of relief at the prospect of being outside, and several shuddered that we could only get out by continuing single file, crouching, being squeezed by the stones and nudged by the person behind. At last we were out in the open, the sun above, and the grass under our feet. Liz and Josie were long gone down the hill, so Jenni and I walked together down the slope toward the car.

"Eww, I felt like I was being squeezed in there in that room," she said.

"Do you want to know why I think the Neolithic people built Newgrange, and what was going on?" I asked.

"Sure."

Lowering my voice to a tone of mystery, I explained my personal theory, "The Neolithic people who built Newgrange five thousand years ago were early agriculturalists. Up until then, people in the Mesolithic era fed themselves by hunting and gathering. These new farmers were intensely aware of fertility, their own, for domesticated livestock, and for the seeds and plants. They believed, as many cultures have, that the earth was the Great Mother nourishing all life. The druids and priests were responsible for understanding the stars, planets, and cycles of the moon, and how they signified the seasons for planting and harvesting. I believe Newgrange was their astronomical observatory, and the symbols incised on the rocks, while beautiful, were instructional manuals for the heavens."

So far I hadn't strayed from at least one expert's studies.

My tone of voice dropped a register to signal the profoundness of my own secret opinion, "But what I also think was going on was that Newgrange was built as the womb of the Mother Earth, domed in pregnancy; that the passage we just crept down was the vagina, as in being reborn; the chambers with their sacred basins were the ovaries; and the central room with the corbelled roof was the uterus. The sky was the Father with his phallic beam of light. Once a year he penetrated the Mother Earth with a shaft of sunlight that reached the interior, swept across the ovarian rooms, across the symbol of the sacred spiral of life in the central chamber, and with that miraculous spark reanimated the earth, as well as the ashes of the dead in the basins to ensure their everlasting life."

I paused, filled with wonder, and looked over at Jenni to see what she thought of the depth of my wisdom.

She looked back at me nodding and said, "Yeah, seventeen minutes, that's about right!"

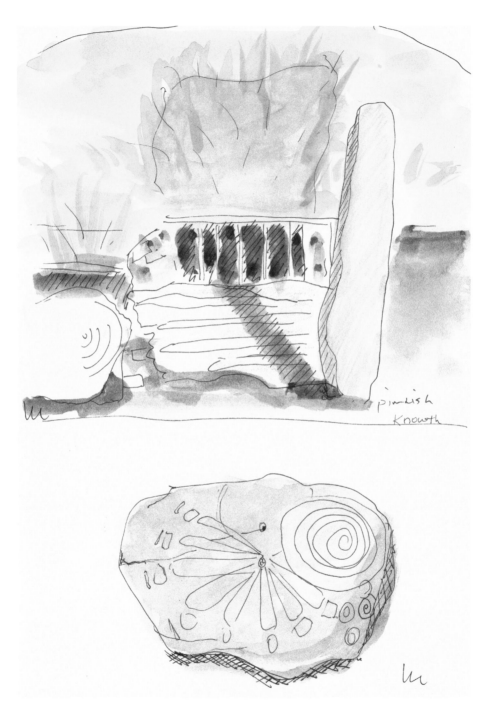

Calendar stones at Knowth.

Chapter XI

Knowth

Still Thursday 19 April

DOWN THE SLOPE WE WALKED in the sunshine. There we found Liz and Josie at the car park where we boarded the van for the return trip to the visitor center and further afield to Knowth, an even larger earthen complex nearby.

Groomed gravel pathways wound steeply up and around seventeen brilliant green mounds surrounding the main mound at Knowth. Knowth is a bright green grass cap resting on a circle of gigantic stone teeth inscribed in otherworldly symbols. It is forty feet high and two hundred and twenty feet in diameter. It is written that more than a third of the total of megalithic art in Western Europe is found at Knowth. A huge stone pillar in front of a black hole in the hill cast a shadow across radiating daisy-like petals carved on the rocky floor. The primary rounded structures were built around five thousand years ago. They were not habitations at that time, but seem to me to have been instructional and ceremonial centers. Added in later eras were burial cists, ring forts, and underground stone-lined pits called souterrains that had been used for long-term underground food storage.

When it comes to prehistory maybe it's just as well to not have been educated, because it's difficult to have an open mind. No one, not even experts, can know for sure how people looked, thought or used an artifact unless there was a record left. And if there was a known record, then it was not prehistoric, since that means *before history was recorded*.

Museums and books about the Stone Age, Paleolithic, and Mesolithic eras sometimes get things wrong. And unfortunately once something is written

people tend to believe it. The written word has an undeserved reputation of credibility and truth. How do I know that? I read it in a book. No, I didn't. To learn something about prehistory, stubbornly resist information as presented, question everything, use intuition and try to think with a fresh mind.

For example, I think about those museum dioramas of cave men and women depicted with dirty, messy hair, slouching around with a club, saying, "Ugh." How wrong that may be. Imagine instead strong young men and women beautifully coiffed with fantastic objects and feathers to hold carefully combed and groomed hair, wearing clothing decorated with shells, small bones, seeds, and feathers over their scented, tattooed, or ochered skin. Imagine them speaking full sentences to each other. Since that is how people of many primitive societies have been actually seen or described, it's at least as plausible than whoever came up with the version we're usually presented.

It's important for me to abandon my assumptions and examine and identify my cultural biases before making guesses about prehistoric people, objects or buildings. The words used to describe prehistory may lead the unwary into those assumptions. Take, for example, the word *cruciform* to describe the three-chambered termination at the end of the tunnel inside a mound such as Newgrange. It makes it sound like a cross, and cross makes it sound Christian, which, of course, has nothing to do with these buildings constructed three thousand years before Christ was born.

Or another example is that because some human remains were found inside and near the mounds, they came to be called tombs. Experts still call them passage tombs, but those words may be powerfully misleading. The term causes the trusting to think that these were built for the purpose of burial. But that is not why I think they were built. Even the word *art* to describe the stone etchings at Knowth, and elsewhere in the world, must be questioned. I wouldn't call it art in a decorative way or even as a skill in doing something. Motif, symbol, or logo may be more accurate than the word art.

What event or belief caused people to build on such a massive scale for ceremonial or instructional purposes? Why were huge complexes such as Stonehenge and Avebury Henge in England, and Newgrange-Knowth-Dowth in Ireland built? Places as far flung as Central America and Egypt built high

towers and pyramids around the same time, about five thousand years ago.

I thought about what these places have in common. *The sky.* I began to search for volcanic eruptions of Icelandic Hekla in that time frame and came across a paper being presented at that time at Oxford University that described two comets, Encke and Oljato, that collided around five thousand five hundred to five thousand years ago. The Earth passed through that asteroid swarm complex, the debris field of the collision, causing several major meteor impacts that triggered additional volcanic activity, tsunamis, and general worldwide mayhem. The growth rings of ancient Irish oaks taken from the bogs show severely limited growth 6370, 5195, 3628 and 3159 years ago. For three years following spring 3159 years ago, tree rings showed no growth, only darkness. For eighteen more years, only small growth lines indicated semi-darkness. Civilizations collapsed, stories of floods and pestilence were likely added to oral histories and mythology.

Northwest Knowth stone

These celestial events could explain the building of the megaliths, the symbols incised on the stones surrounding them, and the intense interest in astronomy. I think the structures were built to study the sky, in part, to anticipate comet strikes, and to worship in such a way as to prevent them in the future.

In the documentary, *Cave of Forgotten Dreams*, Werner Herzog films the extraordinary cave interiors and paintings made thirty thousand years ago in Chauvet, France. One expert in the film, after touring the cave, remarked that Homo Sapiens, *thinking humans*, had been misnamed by the anthropologists. He said, modern people should more appropriately be called *Homo Spiritualis*. I found that interesting. He had seen ritual and ceremony in the paintings of animals in hunt scenes intended to bring about a successful hunt. These humans believed they would change the outcome of their future through rituals performed in the cave. It might not have been so different for the people of five thousand years ago performing rituals they believed would protect them from the comets they could see hurtling their way.

People of the megaliths, as early farmers, may have felt spiritually compelled to make offerings in their worship of the sun, rain, seeds, and seasons in order to bring about another successful planting. But to propitiate the gods, had they sacrificed humans as well? I was thinking about those triple-chambered rooms at the end of a long twisty channel as the reproductive organs of the feminine Earth. In each of the two chambers representing the ovaries were basins with round stone balls, and ashes of human remains. I don't think they were burying people. Instead they may have cremated them elsewhere, reserving the ashes and bones that were ground ritually in the basins and offered up to ensure the safety of the community, and fertility as well as a good crop in the future year. Human sacrifice may have occurred.

As we walked around the site of Knowth, I saw ritual sex where others were too polite or prudish to recognize it and speak about it. I saw phalluses, vaginas, mounds of venus, and labia mixed with calendars, symbols, and maps within the landscape and the sky. It was incredibly interesting.

Leslie walking in the timber henge at Knowth.

South from the Lia Fail — Hill of Tara, Ireland

Two hawthorns on the Hill of Tara.

CHAPTER XII

THE HILL OF TARA

OUR GROUP WAS CALLED to return to the visitor center at Newgrange.

We were off for the Hill of Tara, legendary seat of the high kings of Ireland, and were soon winding our way through the Boyne Valley. I remember a scene from *Gone with the Wind*. Scarlett O'Hara's father is galloping along on his horse over the green fields of his beloved Tara outside of Atlanta, Georgia. He fails to clear a fence, takes a terrific fall, and dies. It was perhaps at the romantic age of fourteen when I first read that book and envisioned the farm and the faraway land in Ireland after which it was named. These green fields now stretched around me.

Embedded in and among the hills, rivers, and valleys were megalithic monuments like Newgrange, Iron Age hill forts, and Uisneach, a ceremonial hilltop at a location that was thought to be the center, or naval, of the country. It was the place for lighting the annual bonfires. Ancient roads linked the sites. Were we on one?

Parked, we wound past the most recent addition to the Hill of Tara, a statue of Saint Patrick who brought Christianity to Ireland in the AD 400s. We continued up the hill past a fort and arrived at the oldest structure, the Mound of the Hostages, a megalith constructed four thousand years earlier when the ancient ones ruled Ireland. Walking on, we found the unabashedly phallic Lia Fail, the Irish *Stone of Destiny*, standing proud on the hilltop. Like a hundred kings before me, and thousands of tourists, I touched it to see if it would cry out a tremendous wail proclaiming me King of Ireland. It did not. Unrecognized, I wandered over to a pair of auspicious hawthorn trees flying bits of ribbon in the breeze. They seemed like an old married couple, intertwined, looking out over the vast plains below. I drew them.

It's all simply too much to take in. History, lore, mythology and songs tell the stories everywhere in Ireland. Scratch the surface of a bit of information to uncover layers and layers of meaningful connections to people, plants and animals, the land, and to each other through time and place. My sisters and I looked south to the lower hill, the Rath-Laoghaire from whom we may be descended through the Quinlan line of our Irish heritage.

Josie, Leslie, and Jenni on the Mound of the Hostages at the Hill of Tara.

In a few moments more, I was going to walk on the Hill of Tara. During my studies I learned the hill had been the home or ceremonial center of at least a hundred and forty-seven early kings, neither divine nor hereditary, but chosen, in the Irish system.

We retraced our footsteps to the car and set off for Trim Castle in the fading light. It was occupied in the Norman era of AD 1172 by its original owner, French Lord Hugh de Lacy, and later taken over by English lords. It was eventually abandoned in the 1600s. It fell to ruin, but remained intact enough that part of the movie

Braveheart was filmed here. Finally we ate well at the Trim Castle Hotel, and made it to our lodging at Mornington House after dark. Although we had no trouble, it is inadvisable to drive after dark on the roads of Ireland. They're often wet, single track, lack roadside lighting, have stray cows and sheep, and are bounded by stone walls with no escape routes. Most cars in Ireland are straight-sided, small, and missing a mirror.

As we said goodnight, Ann O'Hara explained how Warwick couldn't peel a potato; although he brought her a steak after milking three hundred cows. Oh well, she didn't think the girl who came to help at Mornington House was going to work out as she had arrived late.

"Frankly, we can do without her altogether!" She said. "I didn't like her anyway."

LIA FÁIL   HILL OF TARA

The Lia Fail on the Hill of Tara.

At the entrance of a megalith at Loughcrew.

Chapter XIII

Loughcrew

Friday 20 April
Mornington House

THIS HAS BEEN A DAY OF REST and catching up. We walked to Weir's Pub for Josie's Guinness and lunch. The post office was next to the pub so I stopped in for stamps. The attendant handed them over the counter. I left and entered the pub, one door down. There, the post office attendant was serving Josie a Guinness. I smiled. I didn't ask if I could have bought my stamps with my soup.

We learned from the O'Haras that an extensive undeveloped megalithic cairn system, Loughcrew, was nearby. They said it was gated, but we would be able to ask for the key from Loughcrew Gardens. Thirty-five minutes later we picked up the key to the Calendar Temple ruins with instructions for where to walk, and cautions regarding the structure itself. It was strange to let ourselves in to this property on private land and make our own way around these ancient mounds. The entrance to one was dark, small and creepy, with stones incised with similar patterns found at Newgrange.

We four each took a turn crouching low at the entrance, stuck our head into the dark tunnel, and refused to go further. Without a guide this place was decidedly spooky. Loughcrew was built five thousand years ago. Also called the Hill of the Witches, thirty "tombs" stretched across three hilltops. The Hay and Fairy Queen was mistress to all Ireland. I've since learned the complex contains two hundred decorated stones, a main mound, and seventeen smaller mounds.

Although it's undeveloped, it is the most extensive megalithic site in Ireland and related to other sites of the Boyne River area. All the sites have solar and lunar orientations and work together across the Irish landscape to predict equinoxes, solstices and quarter days.

Upon our return to the house, we were treated to an excellent supper of blue cheese soufflé, beef and Guinness, beets, and lettuce and pea soup. The table was beautifully set with multi-armed candelabras on either side of us as we dined. Ann came and went from the kitchen pushing the swinging door open with her chair. We spoke of our day and were entertained by Ann O'Hara's dark observations of her life, friends, and family.

She told us of those unwed mothers, the laundresses of Madeline, they all sent their linens to them back then, but never *realized!* Of course she counseled the girl at work about her pregnancy, her parents were dead, her aunt and uncle and cousin were taking care of her, but they kicked her out after she told them about it, gave up the child, etc., etc.

Trying to make polite conversation, one of us remarked on the portrait of a man high on the dining room wall.

"Oh, he was a dead solider, the short one who lived," she explained. "The two tall ones before and after, got killed, but he was short enough, pulling that cable, you know, to live."

Ann continued about her relative who fought in World War I who wrote home to say he thought he was going to survive his minor wound, but he died. And with deep satisfaction, she told us of her great-great-grandfather who died at thirty-two years of age leaving his will to be contested.

Thinking there could be no more terrible news for the evening, we were surprised by her final observation about John Michelhenny, the Tobasco Tycoon. He had kicked all the tenants off his estate, and Ann described how these poor native Irish moaned and keened up and down the street as their homes were being destroyed.

After dinner I paused to show Ann the little study guide I had compiled for our group. She let me know, "No time to look at your little book, got to go!" At that she wheeled off for bed.

Saturday 21 April
Mornington House

This morning we planned to have a driver take us in to Dublin to visit the archeology museum and spend time in the National Library researching our family background. Before we could be on our way, Ann treated us to the reason she didn't do breakfast—she couldn't get in the oven. She also described how she looked over at the lump in the bed next to her and wondered if her husband wouldn't get up and get her a cup of tea.

Our clerk at the National Library looked like our cousin in Michigan, Norton. Books in hand, we sat in the reading room at tables with green-shaded lamps feeling fusty indeed. There was not enough time to learn much.

Daunted by the amount of research needed, we went off to the horse races in Naas.

Jenni, Leslie, Josie, and Liz at the Naas horse race.

Our driver stayed with the car while we went in for lunch and to learn how to place our bets. We each chose our horse to bet on by liking its name, or the colors of the silks the jockeys wore. But not Jenni.

When I asked her later about her favorite memories of the trip, she recalled, "Oh, I loved the horse racing! Did you see those jockeys? They looked like they were twelve years old, and not because they were small! They looked like kids! I really liked to walk around inside the paddock with the horses, owners, and jockeys where I looked at the conformation of each of the horses. That's how I picked my horse. And I picked the driver's horse!"

I love the way memory works. I remembered we chose the gift for the driver, by placing a bet on a horse named Eriagon because the jockey and horse silks were the same colors as our van. We plunked down our money, traipsed outside to the rail of the paddock to watch the action.

Josie, Liz, and our driver.

And we're off to the horse race in Naas.

Horses and riders in matching silks pranced around to line up. And they're off! We four lost, but our bet for our driver won big with twenty-five to one. After the race, the horses and jockeys mingled with owners and well-wishers. We saw a Blackwater Stud sign on a horse trailer. It was great viewing, and our driver was delighted by his surprise win.

Back home, I failed to record the details of the night's meal, probably because it was lamb, which I detest, but remembered to jot down the last of Ann O'Hara's downers. Asked if the lamb was local, she said, no, the last spring lamb of theirs went to market in 1978. The next day we were heading north to Bushmill's Inn in County Antrim, so she made sure we knew they didn't have a ramp and were hardly wheelchair accessible. She said it was like at the opera where she was put on a platform, *above* everyone else in the *back*. Lastly, I chose an apron I brought from America to give to her, as I had each of the lodging owners with whom we stayed. I knew Ann took pride in her cooking.

"Thanks for everything," I said, handing her the apron.

She immediately tossed it aside saying, "I'll just put it in with the thousand other aprons we have."

Wow, ouch.

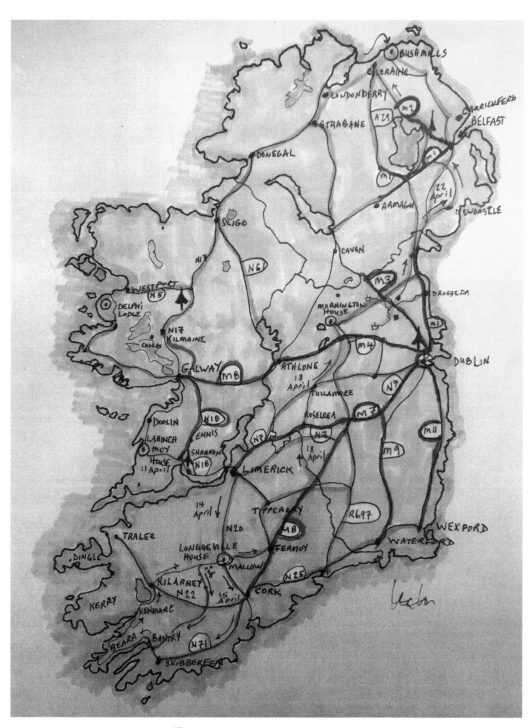

DRIVING MAP 22 APRIL

Chapter XIV

Finding Our Father's Line

The time may come to let it go to Mother Earth.
If this should pass, where once were walls, I'll rest amid
the stones, without a roof, the rain will fall soft on
my face, the wind, where windows were, will freely breathe
the sweetgrass scented air, and memories will live.

~Leslie Lee, *Sacred Space*

Sunday 22 April
From Mornington House, Co. Meath
To Bushmills Inn Hotel
9 Dunluce Road, Bushmills, Co. Antrim

We Took Leave of Mornington House as we headed for Northern Ireland after breakfast. Goodbye, Ann, goodbye, Warwick.

As a visitor to Ireland, I hardly think I'm qualified to comment on the conflicts between Northern Ireland and the Republic of Ireland, however some mention must be made so tourists like us will have enough sensitivity to not offend the residents of either side. I found it best to make no comment, or to listen politely while reserving my opinions until I knew someone well enough to

ask questions. The primary conflict within Northern Ireland has been between native Irish Catholics and Protestant English and Scots who emigrated there when England colonized much of the Province of Ulster. The issues centered on the Irish being forced to give up their land and independence. There is a border between the Republic and Northern Ireland I'm thankful is only on a map.

The Republic of Ireland is part of the European Union whose currency is the euro. Northern Ireland is part of the United Kingdom and the EU whose currency is the pound sterling. Northern Ireland has a queen, the Republic of Ireland does not. Both the Republic of Ireland and Northern Ireland have a complicated, divisive history not dealt with here, but most want peace.

After much debate about what could be accomplished on the way between Mullingar and Bushmills, we decided to detour to Castlewellan, the nearest town to the Nixon name I wrote in the margin of my map so many months before regarding our family who may have lived nearby at Ballywillwill, for at least six generations. Last winter Liz punched into the computer the pronunciation the great-granny in the 1950s used when her children asked where the ancestral Scotch-Irish relatives lived. She said, "Bally-well-WELL."

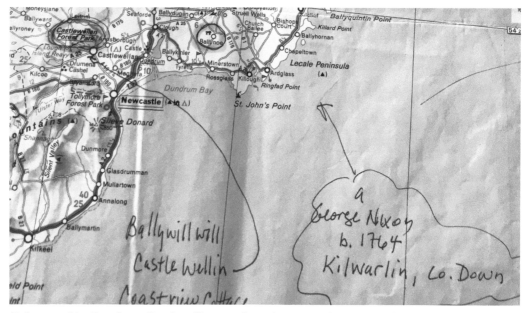

I drew a thin line from Castlewellan out into the sea and wrote, "Nixon. Ballywillwill."

And everyone laughed at her. The computer spit out the answer. It was the townland spelled Ballywillwill, not far from Castlewellan, beautiful Newcastle on the ocean, and the home of the famous Bronte sisters in Rathfriland. How did these Nixons connect with my known family?

I knew my grandmother, Beryl, and my grandfather, Chet Lee, but not their parents. She was a tiny, well-shaped serious-minded Methodist and social worker. He was a rollicking, hard-drinking, intelligent, itinerant woodsman. We later came to know he descended from William Lee of Carrickfergus, Ireland in the 1600s. I will return to how we came to know that later in this story.

I only knew my grandmother's father, James Elmer Niles, as a formal photograph hanging in my entryway at home. My sister Liz and my grandmother both resembled him. His father spirited him away as a baby from the Nixon-Nichols-Niles clan. They were a large loving, perhaps grasping, family who pioneered the territory around Lansing, Michigan in 1836. Heartbroken by the early death of the baby's mother, Louisa Nixon, William Niles fled north with his children to Petoskey. There as a young man, James Elmer Niles met Hannah Peacock Herrington, whose parents settled the area. Their child Beryl Niles was my grandmother.

But let us take one step back from poor Louisa to see how her parents came to Michigan. Louisa never seemed strong among the intrepid families who carved farms from the wilderness of Michigan. Her mother, Annis Nichols, was the prototypical pioneer woman who chopped wood, baked bread, sang songs, shoveled snow and had many successful children. Annis married James Radcliffe Nixon, preacher, who sailed on the Algernon as a child from Northern Ireland. He was born to George and Mary Radcliffe Nixon at Ballywillwill, Northern Ireland. By all accounts, Mary Radcliffe was beloved as a saint. She was described as, "Scotch frugality and vigor, Irish wit, and English perseverance, with courage, industry, and strength of character." After arriving in New York, she and George moved west into Ontario, Canada in a settlement called Canada West. There he died. Mary raised her four sons who all left to claim homestead lands near Lansing, Michigan in 1836. We live two hundred miles north of Lansing now. But we still wondered where was the Ballywillwill of our ancestors in Ireland?

Pulling into the parking lot in front of the butcher shop and post office in Castlewellan, we decided the best strategy was simply to go in and ask around. Josie and I, unlikely to approach a stranger, stayed in the car as usual. Our scouts, Jenni jumped out to head in to the post office, and Liz headed off toward the butcher. What a long shot in learning about our ancestors. None of us expected much out of this strategy, but it was worth a try.

In the post office, Jenni walked up to the line of people waiting for service at the counter and asked, "Have any of you ever heard of the Nixons or Ballywillwill?"

Immediately, one lady at the counter turned to her and said, "I don't know about Ballywillwill, but my husband, Paul Walsh, is from Bally-well-WELL! He's in the car. He can tell us."

The lady brought Jenni out to the car parked right next to ours. She spoke through the window to her husband. Paul Walsh stepped out of the car leaving their children in the back seat.

Josie and I drew near in time to hear him say, "Why, Bobby Nixon! I grew up across the street from him at Bally-well-WELL just down the road. I can take you there, it's just a moment's drive."

Well, WELL, blow our socks off! Our family records claiming the mythical place had been a joke pulled on the great granny was so wrong. By now, Liz rejoined our group. We excitedly told him the story of our family search for the legendary Ballywillwill.

He said, "It's no trouble, and just a little way. I'll ride with you and my wife will follow in the car."

Meeting in Castlewellan.

He led us over the rolling hills along the small road and turned right at the church.

"That's not your church, but this here is English's pub, your local. You're related to them, well, you're related to most folks around here. Go along another kilometer to Ballywillwill."

Looking left and right at the fields on either side of the road, I asked, "What is a townland?"

He said, "It's a collection of acreage. Ballywillwill used to have more, but the Nixons have thirty-five acres or so. Here you are. No one has lived here at the old place for a long time, so its fallen down, but I've seen one of Bobby's sons here working on the stone wall."

We pulled to the side of the road and climbed out of the van. This was where our forebears raised their children for at least two hundred years.

Oh, it was sweet! Ballywillwill could not have been more charming.

Parked on the side of the road, we picked our way past rutted fields and across a pasture since the driveway was impassable. We walked up the rise in a dream state. A roofless stone cottage surrounded by abandoned stone outbuildings still stood with an intact small stone barn. I felt like I was holding my breath as I peered into windows at the spaces where I imagined family after family living. He pointed out a large stone sink outdoors that was used for retting flax to prepare it for linen making. Oh, it was sweet! The property was left as it was after the Nixon great-grandfather, John, died. Ballywillwill was then passed to his son, George. His son, Bobby, now in his eighties, moved to a small modern house somewhere nearby that he could manage. He then passed it on to his son,

George, of our generation. George lived in County Down, but came here from time to time to rebuild some of the stone fences.

Ballywillwill could not have been more charming with a tiny fallen down house, a small barn steps away, a stream leading past the buildings into the side yard to the closed gate, and a collection of fields beyond.

I stood by the gate turning slowly, taking it all in. Deeply rutted stone wheel tracks ran between shoulder-high hedgerows topped with beautiful flowers, gorse, and hawthorn trees before they disappeared up the rise and around a bend. We regrouped at the gate.

"This used to be the original entrance," Paul Walsh said. "But the little river washed it out in a flood and it hasn't been fixed."

My hand was on the gate. We stood in the shade of the ancient planted hawthorns.

Liz, with reverent nostalgia, softly repeated, "James Nixon, our Michigan relative, James Nixon, James Radcliffe Nixon's family lived right here."

He turned and pointed up the hill, "Well, that's the Radcliffe house right up there on the hill, the last place on the road.

Liz's eyes widened, "James RADCLIFFE Nixon. James RADCLIFFE Nixon. His father, George, and Mary Radcliffe were born and raised here, married, and came to America!"

Paul added, "That's right. Of course, you're related to all the people around here. The Englishes, Radcliffes, and Nixons."

The Radcliffe's white farmhouse and barns were just there on the hill. It was impossible to take it all in. The years that had passed, the people who had braved the new world in America, those parents and grandparents who had stayed behind knowing they would never see their newly-wedded children again. Or those grandchildren. I still tear up at the memory of standing there on this humble family land with Liz, Jenni, and Josie.

Who could have guessed we would ever find our way home? Later in Michigan, none of us could believe how fortunate and fortuitous we had been. It was beyond anything we had dreamed of finding in Ireland.

The Radcliffe farm

Paul then told us how to find the oldest Nixon whose son now owns the cottage. So after handshakes and treats for the patient children and goodbyes to his wife, off we drove to find the address we were given. Thirty minutes later, we pulled into a drive next to a small white house. Jen and Liz, the bold ones, tried the bell and peeked in the windows of the empty house. No luck, but they wanted to cross the road and run up the curving drive to see if any neighbors might know something of the Nixon resident. Time passed while Josie and I waited in the car.

At last, they were bounding across the road, breathlessly telling us that the people living across the road knew a Nixon cousin who lived in Newcastle named Brian Gibson. The neighbors insisted on calling them right away, saying the Gibsons would never forgive them if they let the American cousins get away. He phoned Brian, who insisted that we come by to visit them at home.

Jenni, Brian Gibson, Leslie, and Liz

Address in hand, we found our way into Newcastle and a newer neighborhood of bright, clean, two story homes. Address in hand, we pulled in the drive. In anticipation they called their family members to tell them we were coming. The Gibson grandfather came from next door. What a warm welcome. The grandfather came across the lawn to greet us when he saw us pull in the drive from his house. We piled out of the car to hugs, questions, and exclamations of surprise. Once inside, we were greeted at the door by our cousin, Brian, and his wife who invited us into the living room to sit and tell all about how we had managed to find them.

Liz took the lead while she and the grandfather opened their respective genealogies to our shared pages. Liz unfolded the huge white three ring binder she carried all the way to Ireland.

"Here we are, this is where we match up." Liz said.

Jenni, Grandpa Gibson, Liz, and Leslie

While they looked at the paperwork, we looked around the uncluttered, bright room at the family photographs arrayed on the side tables. There was Jimmy, Liz's middle son, as a ten year old. But it wasn't Jimmy. It was the Gibson's version of Jimmy. We seemed to see Jimmy repeatedly in our travels. He looks just like Prince Harry with his impish smile, strawberry blonde hair and lanky good looks.

Liz quickly established our mutual pedigree by looking at their genealogy and fitting us in while the rest of us chatted and looked at photographs of people who looked a lot like us.

Brian told us that George Nixon, our age, lived in Downpatrick with his wife, Vivienne, another hour away from where we were. He said although George was busy with work he would want to meet us. Brian called George, who insisted we come to meet them. Would we be able to come in two days to Downpatrick? I thought of the long drive to Bushmills in the dark tonight I was facing, just to turn around in two days to make the same drive back. Yes, okay, of course.

It was hard to say goodbye, but the light was fading and we had to get on the road. Amid hugs and waves we boarded the van and were off.

NIL AON TINTEAN NODO TINTEAN FEIN

Ireland   Bushmills 24 April 2007   lee

Chapter XV

William Lee of Carrickfergus

It tiptoes through the ancient streets and courtyards
of an older world to peer into the heart of home—
the single room of hearth and fire, of food and drink,
of songs and tales and families safe from stormy seas.
May every house possess these virtues of a hut.

~Leslie Lee, *Sacred Space*

Monday 23 April
Bushmills Inn Hotel
County Antrim, Northern Ireland

IT WAS A LONG DRIVE back to Bushmills in the dark last night. I was exhausted, my eyes burned by the end of the drive on the seemingly endless winding one-lane roads. We dined in, thank god, with a meal of salmon with cream corn sauce. This inn was quaint, old, and near the ocean. The lobby was a quintessential Irish welcome. The turf and coal fire warmed the tiled entry with a place to sit to shake off the chill and pull off muddy boots before going in to the dining room. Carved on the mantle were these words, *Nil aon tintean mar no do tintean tein. There is no hearth like your own hearth.*

The Bushmills Inn in County Antrim.

I woke up this Monday morning in leisurely fashion, painted drawings with new watercolor pencils before breakfast, then headed down to a grand buffet. It included serving bowls of homemade plain yogurt and various fruit compotes as light as a slurry to drizzle on top, thin slices of ham, and breakfast meats, choices of cheeses, toasts, jams, granolas, and boiled eggs. Whatever juice was favorite, there it was, and coffee, and tea of course.

The Giant's Causeway, a tourist destination, was our first stop of the day. It's an interesting geological formation of a series of large geometric stones stacked on one another large enough to clamber on. From there we walked across a gorge on a harrowing rope bridge at Carrick-a-rede, then on to the Marine Hotel for lunch in Ballycastle. After, we wove up and down hills and in and out coves along the spectacular oceanside Glens of Antrim down to the small city of Carrickfergus.

On this long day of touring the North Coast of Ireland we came close enough to Carrickfergus to make a side trip to visit even though it was late. This was the home of our antique Lee relative on our father's direct line.

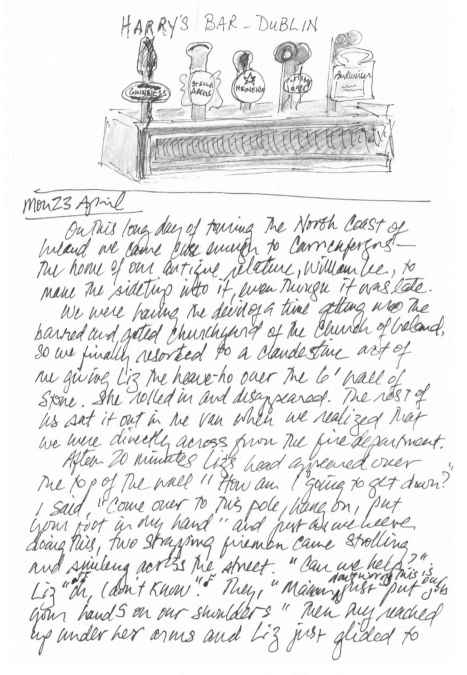

An excerpt from my journal on 23 April.

Before we left America, Liz found a distant cousin who was directly descended from our mutual great grandfather. She asked him to take a genetic test. The results of his test and our genealogy plugged into the computer informed Liz we are directly descended from a William Lee of Carrickfergus, Ireland in the 1600s. What an amazing coincidence.

In another bizarre twist before we left for Ireland, a neighbor called me in my tiny village in Michigan.

"Hi, my name is Stephen Lee. We've never met, but you know my wife Kathy from the elementary school. We live just over on Pine, a few blocks from you."

"Oh, hi, sure, I know Kathy," I said.

Stephen continued, "I know you were in business for yourself and I had a question."

We chatted awhile and just as we were signing off he asked me an interesting question.

"Say, my last name is Lee, and your last name is Lee and I was just wondering if we might be related?"

I thought that was stretching it for someone I'd never met in this town of eight hundred residents.

"Well, not unless you're descended from William Lee of Carrickfergus, Ireland of the 1600s," I said.

There was a pause.

He said, "I'm directly descended from William Lee of Carrickfergus, Ireland and I have the genealogy."

"Would you be willing to take a genetic test?" I said, stunned. "I've bought them for everyone in my family, but we don't have a decisive genealogical connection to this William Lee. That would be a huge confirmation. Oh, my sister Liz is going to be so excited."

I ordered the test to be sent directly to Stephen, he offered to have his Aunt Cindy, his family's genealogist, lend him the thick book of ancestry. I arranged to have Liz visit with the test results she had from the distant male cousin, and we agreed to meet to compare results and check out the genealogy.

The day we were to meet Stephen for the first time arrived with much

anticipation. Liz drove an hour from her Petoskey home with the earlier genetic test results and what little she knew of the line. We settled in. Stephen came to the door, his face resembling my grandfather, Chet Lee, from Petoskey. We greeted each other like cousins.

After settling in with beverages, we stood at the end of the counter in my kitchen. Stephen brought out the results from testing with FamilyTreeDNA. He smoothed open the paperwork with its matrix of numbers and letters indicating the mutations in the Lee lineage. Liz opened her paperwork. We held our breath. Were we about to gain another cousin on the Lee side? We only had two female cousins from our father's sister. It seemed impossible for this new technology to attach a living man to one who died almost four hundred years ago. We buzzed with excitement.

"Let's see if they match," I said.

I took the papers from Liz and read the first set of numbers out loud.

"Check." Stephen said.

I read the next set. "Check."

We looked up at each other as we read, making sounds of sharp inhalations, and "oh, oh, my" with each result.

"Check, check."

I read the numbers from all of the boxes, all twelve checked exactly the same. We beamed at each other. Cousins! My father died when we were in our twenties, his father was gone, we had so few male family members on the Lee side. Until now.

"Let's look at the genealogy!" Liz took the tome into her hands, and eagerly poured over the contents quickly finding where our paths diverged.

"See here, the Lees were together outside of Indianapolis in Boone County. Your side of the family stayed in Indiana, and our line moved north to Petoskey, Michigan." Liz said.

"And this other line went with the Mormons to Utah with Brigham Young. His offspring, Harold Lee, eventually became the head of the Church. That's how we know about William Lee of Carrickfergus, Ireland. The Mormons had to *seal his record*, that involved knowing every birth and death of his genealogy." Stephen explained.

I was amazed to know how it all fit, and I was delighted to have a Lee cousin. Liz and I were happy to confirm the connection we've enjoyed since.

Back in Ireland with the sisters we stopped at the heritage center in Carrickfergus to ask about records for the Lees.

"Hi, we're trying to find any records on the William Lee family."

"Oh, the Mormons stole them a long time ago," the curator said.

How ironic. The installation of Harold Lee as the head of the Mormon Church in the 1950s prompted the alleged theft of our family papers.

After failing at records, we decided to search for gravestones in the cemetery. Slightly after hours, we had a devil of a time getting into a barred and gated churchyard of the Church of Ireland standing on a hill in the middle of the town of Carrickfergus. We finally resorted to a clandestine act. I gave Liz the heave-ho over the six foot wall of stone. Liz stepped into my hands, grasped the bars of the fence, stepped up onto my shoulder, and up onto the ledge flinging her leg over the rail. She rolled in and disappeared. The rest of us sat it out in the van or loitered on the sidewalk when we realized that we were directly across from the fire department with several officials standing on the sidewalk watching our activities.

After twenty minutes Liz's head appeared over the top of the wall, "Pssst! How am I going to get down?"

"Come over to this pole, hang on, step on my shoulder and put your foot in my hand," I said. Just as we were doing this, two strapping fireman came strolling and smiling across the street. Uh-oh! Josie and I looked at each other.

"Busted!"

The firemen smiled, "Can we help?"

"Oh, I don't know," Liz said coyly.

"Ma'am don't worry, this is our job. Just give us your hands."

Delighted, Liz reached down. They lifted their hands up under her arms and Liz glided to the ground.

"Oh, thank you, you're so strong, how did you do that?" Liz cooed.

They were quite handsome. We thanked them and took pictures together. We asked Liz what she had found on the other side of the iron fence in the graveyard. Sadly she found nothing useful.

The return to Bushmills was exhausting in the dark and mist. Distances in Ireland don't convey the time it takes to travel them.

DRIVING MAP 23 APRIL

Here we are in Castlewellan — the small town closest to our Nixon family homestead in Ballywillwill — pronounced Ballywellwell, not far from the beautiful Newcastle on the ocean. This is the town where we met Paul Walsh who grew up across from Bobby Nixon and took us to "our" old farmstead. So, Today, we met our cousin George Nixon who owns the property and is

Lamps at the inn in Castlewellan where we stopped for tea. Excerpted from my journal.

CHAPTER XVI

COUSINS

Then we go home to watch a patch of sun explore
the floor, or learn to build a fortress against time
with books and secret places of imagining,
or find a way to heal in havens of retreat,
and thank our line of ancestors who brought us here.

~Leslie Lee, *Sacred Space*

Tuesday 24 April
Bushmills Inn Hotel
County Antrim

DOWNPATRICK IS A TOWN NESTLED IN THE HILLS and shaded by enormous oak trees where the body of Saint Patrick lies interred in the churchyard. A river flows out to the sea via Strangford Lough on which the Nixon's house was connected. It was a smuggler's hideout hundreds of years ago. They showed us around the beautiful, rambling house and yard where they raised their family. We were welcomed into the large, warm kitchen where George and Vivienne made us comfortable with tea and cakes from the Aga stove. An Aga brand, glistening enamel in a variety of colors, is the epitome of Irish kitchen comfort and durability. Once lit, an Aga remains on forever warming and drying the damp climate. We sat around the long wood table.

George was slender, tall, and dark with a wide generous smile and a look of mystification. Vivienne was fair, slight, and spoke quietly. We talked and talked. Now they were retired, and the children away, they were selling this house to rebuild the family homestead at Ballywillwill to live in. Was I a little jealous? Yes, and grateful to have seen it in its original state before it changed. And I was grateful to know it would be cared for well into the future.

"How could you possibly have found us?" George asked.

We explained the odyssey of how it all started in Michigan, through our chance meeting of Paul Walsh in Castlewellan at the post office, our tour of precious Ballywillwill, the trip to the elder Nixon house and meeting those neighbors, discovering the Gibsons, and how that led us to them in Downpatrick. We all sat back amazed.

Then George asked, "Did you say Paul Welsh?"

"No, Paul Walsh," I said.

"Well, that explains it then," George said. "I've been looking for him for a year to hire him to repair some stone walls out at Ballywillwill, but had the name wrong and wasn't able to reach him."

I asked him with a smile, "Would you like his phone number?"

George said, "Oh, yes!" And we laughed.

Still Tuesday 24 April

We were off to Navan Fort, also called Emain Macha, the royal site of the kings of Ulster. Haughey's Fort, two miles from Emain Macha, has high embankments, deep ditches, pools and large dogs. It was first occupied during the climate disaster 3166 years ago.

We came upon a group of people with a donkey standing in the road on our way through the countryside. They moved to the side to let us through. We asked what they were doing. They explained they were road bowling. This game involved long stretches of road and heavy steel balls that were flung. Needless to say we had never heard of road bowling. Where did they get steel balls? What were the rules? It did make me wonder if people in cars were struck by a stray steel ball as they came around the corner.

Jenni's Words of the Day:
"Cary Grant was tall!" Liz said.
"Yeah, he's always been tall." Jenni marveled.

At Navan Fort, also called Emain Macha, the royal site of the kings of Ulster.

Wednesday 25 April
Bushmills Inn Hotel

After an early breakfast, we were off for Donegal. At Dunfanaghan of the blowhole, we lunched. The scenery was becoming spectacular. Liz remembered this remarkable coastline as one of her favorites. There was some confusion regarding directions around Horn Head, and we landed in someone's yard. Then out to the beautiful "Bloody Foreland" through the peat fields and barrens. On the other side, the coast was developed with holiday cottages. We dined at the Harbor Restaurant. St. Ernan's in Donegal earned a star in my notes, but I no longer remember why. We drove home to Bushmills at the end of a long day.

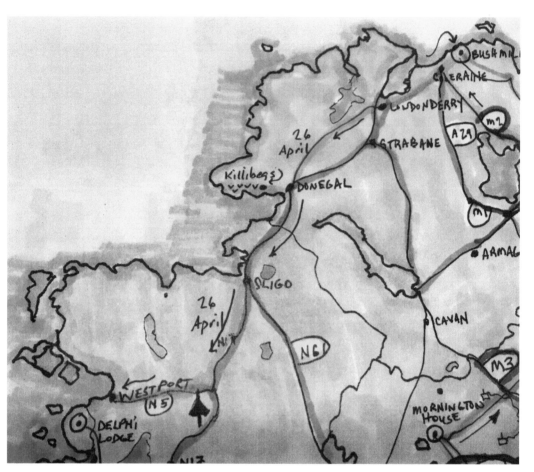

DRIVING MAP FOR 26 APRIL

Chapter XVII

The Cliffs of Sliabh Liag

Thursday 26 April
From Bushmills in Co. Antrim
To Delphi Lodge
Leenane, Co. Galway

We Shopped, And Sadly Left this charming place. Our host, Brian, couldn't have been nicer. After driving to the west coast, we bought gifts at the famous Magee's in Donegal until three p.m. when we went out to see the cliffs past Killibegs on the peninsula. These, the Sliabh Liag, are the highest sea cliffs in Europe.

It was only when I could not see the road, but only the sky, that I became truly alarmed at the vertical climb up the edge on a single lane dirt road. When I saw only sky I automatically braked. The ascent was so steep I was afraid to take my foot off the brakes and petrified we would begin sliding back to plunge off the cliff edge backward. I was terrified the road in front of us turned so sharply that if I moved forward we'd dive over a precipice. Would the transmission hold? We were in a minivan, not an SUV. We hung in our vehicle staring at the blue sky. It was untenable. With my left foot securely on the brake pedal, I slid my right foot to hover over the accelerator. I would do my best to lift the brake exactly at the same time as I gently pressed the gas.

The front of the van tipped forward like a seesaw into the void. For that split second of weightlessness I felt we had pitched off the cliff.

"Oh, my gahhhd! Where is the road?!" My mind screamed.

Front wheels ground into the gravel. We fell forward in our seats toward the immense blue ocean roaring almost two thousand feet below us. It was like the scariest part of the roller coaster when the track drops away and the stomach lifts into the throat. Both feet braked hard, the front wheels found the grit. Heart pounding, I refocused. I imagined the van as a space traveler that was untethered from the mother ship sailing out over the great blue void. *Noooo!* Beads of moisture popped out on my upper lip. The two-track snaked around the cliff to the right. We crept forward around a blind curve trusting that beyond the ten feet bit of road I could see in front of our car, there would be more road.

There was more road. It widened and flattened out in a dome ever falling away to the ocean below. It was a parking area of sorts. There, we bailed from the car. I tried to walk around on jellified knees until the adrenaline subsided. My vertigo prompted me to scream silently at my family, *You're too close to the edge! Where are the rails?* We peered off into crevasses of distant pools of trapped surf. Out over the rise of the cliff we had driven up lay the Atlantic Ocean, vast, deep

blue to the far horizon. The views from above were beyond spectacular. But perhaps not worth our lives.

Mountain climbers and hikers know it's harder to descend than ascend. I was likewise afraid of the return trip and at our current pace, we were not going to make dinner at the Delphi Lodge. I worried what would happen if we met another car. There was no place to turn, no way out but forward. It was time to face our departure. With deep breathing we strapped ourselves into the ineffectual seatbelts for the thirty-minute ride down. Just as we were about to round the first bend, the hood of a vehicle rose into view. I was so glad we met it at the top. In the mountains it's always the driver pointing downhill who must reverse to a place of turn around. I backed up. I wondered how many wrecked cars…? *No*. We proceeded down slowly without incident.

To make time, we cut across the County Mayo peninsula to drop into the wild and beautiful northern mountains of the Connemara. It's a place out of time, out of the past, out of the modern era. The rising of vast moors to misty rocky peaks without a human trace but the diminishing road made my heart hurt. Were there really places so remote in Ireland? Yes. And low along the valleys the streams of water feeding into rivers opening into lochs led us to the Delphi Lodge. It was built in the 1880s as a remote hideaway for fishing sportsmen. The gravel drive led to a woodsy parking area where cars tucked in between tree trunks. Dragging our bags across the gravel, we crossed the stone sill through the red door. Ahhhh, a lovely, comfortable home.

CHAPTER XVIII

DELPHI LODGE

As life on Earth in all its forms first flows through plants
So as we flow, a fallen leaf in gentle dew,
or swiftly down the stream, or trapped against the rocks,
and as the water seeks the sea, we hope to find
cerulean peace and oneness in the silent deep.

~Leslie Lee, *Sacred Space*

Thursday 26 April
Delphi Lodge Arrival

"SORRY YOU'VE MISSED DINNER, but let me show you around."

The kind lady set us up with soup and salmon in the library, showed us how to help ourselves to coffee in the kitchen, toured us around the snooker table room with the honor bar, then helped drag my suitcase up the long staircase while I pushed.

"We're not a hotel, and don't have bellboys, but we're all happy to help." She said as she dragged the front half of my bag up the staircase as I lifted the back. She went on, "Books stay in the library, and drinks must be noted in the booze book. Plenty of hunting and fishing books. Delphi Lodge is not, and does not pretend to be, a hotel. It has no room service. It is first and foremost a private country house, complete with smelly dogs, an occasionally presumptuous child, and a degree of attendant chaos."

"We hope you'll relax in the house-party atmosphere, regarding yourself as a personal guest of the family. If there is anything we can do for you, simply ask Peter or one of the staff. There's no choice of menu, but the cook can arrange for something if you have a special request or diet. We assume you will eat with us unless you tell us differently that morning. Unless such notice is given we must charge you since the food will otherwise be prepared unnecessarily. Breakfast is between nine and ten a.m."

In the welcome packet I found the rules:

Dogs other than ours not allowed
No feeding the dogs or let them follow on walks
No snooker after midnight (or for under sixteens)
No fishing rods or boots in bedrooms
Shut all gates securely
No visiting the salmon hatchery unaccompanied
TV- don't encourage it, fight staff for channel changer
No wake up calls
Check out 11 a.m.
Tips tin in office: 10pp per night average, all tips are shared out
Tips fishing guide: 10 per half day session if happy, or more

Our rooms were comfortable, yet spare. No locks, as I found out when a man opened my door while I sat naked on the floor unpacking. For drinks we gathered around seven-thirty p.m. in the library before dinner at eight p.m.

A fisherman on the river near the Delphi Lodge.

Friday 27 April (early)
Delphi House

The lodge was in charge of assigning guests to sections of river or loch from a boat with a gillie as a guide. The best stretches to assign guests may have been decided through a lottery system.

We woke early to a sunny morning. I helped myself to tea in the kitchen. On our way out for a long walk down to the tranquil Doo Loch, we crossed under the trees into the parking lot. There we were treated to watch the custom of each fishermen standing at the trunk of his car, suiting up in waders, pulling out gear, showing off flies, and preparing for a day on the water.

The yearling salmon are released from their tank into the sea loch.

We arrived back at the lodge in time to see several men with a red tractor backing a tank to the edge of the water and dumping it in. We asked what was happening and were delighted to discover we were witnessing the annual fingerling salmon release. The lodge operates a hatchery down the lane (don't let the dog follow you) where they raise the salmon. A fin of each fish is clipped so when they're caught by the lodgers in the streams and lochs, Delphi Lodge knows if it was one of theirs returning from the ocean to spawn.

Josie and I sat on the end of the dock for an hour watching the little fish react to their newly found freedom. They leapt up, twisted their little bodies while looking wildly around before falling back into the loch. There were as many as a dozen fish flinging themselves out at the same time across the surface of the lake. Peering into the water, we could see the five-inch long fish finding each other, grouping up in clusters, and heading out to the mouth of the river. Fascinating! How do they know? It is incredible to me that their one-year-old instincts tell them exactly what to do having only known life in a tank up to then. Is our search for home so different, a vestige of a deeper, cellular level compulsion?

In the future, if I'm lucky enough to return, I want it to be on the day the salmon are released. It was so joyful watching the baby fish find their freedom. They seemed to have emotions and showed how excited they were. On top of that they mystically seem as if they know where they're going and know what to do. We followed the tractor up to the fishery to learn about the process. The dogs were already there, honest.

Later, I drove down to the beaches to watch the surfing and to mail my accumulated books at the post office. Why had I never imagined surfing in Ireland? As an island with huge exposure to the prevailing winds of the Atlantic Ocean, I should have guessed. I'd seen surfers during our travels along the south and west shoreline on many beaches dotting the ocean in black skin suits guarding against the cold. Some of the beaches were wide and deep, as near Sligo. Others, as off Doolin in County Clare, were incredibly treacherous with huge waves breaking onto towering rocky shorelines with only a small safe landing.

I was back in time to shower and dress for drinks and dinner. We were in our glory surrounded by so many enchanting men chatting about fishing, their gillies, and the sections of river and loch they'd been on for the day. One charming lodge guest, an important person in the Church of Ireland, was celebrating his sixty-ninth birthday and was a grand storyteller. Liz was in her glory and remembered this, as we all did, as a highlight of the trip. Other guests were luminaries as well. They included an economist from Inverness, a Man Booker Prize winner, a Paisley government official, married radiologists, and an author and his friend. None of the guests were arrogant or lofty, and easy conversation and laughter ranged pleasantly around the long table.

When it was my turn to add in, I began the story of our recent experience visiting Newgrange much the same way it is written in this journal. I sensed the table quieting, and heads turning to me as I related my unusual opinions about why it had been built and how it was used.

"We were excited to be able to get tickets to go inside Newgrange, the six thousand year old passage tomb, a few days ago. Everyone calls it a passage tomb, but after reading about it, and then going inside, I don't think it was used for burial. I don't know if you've ever been in there, but you creep in down a long, twisted passage to end up in a domed room with a corbelled ceiling that you can stand up in. Chambers open up left, right, and center with strange basins with stone balls, and inscribed symbols."

"As you probably know, the window over the tunnel allows a sunbeam to shine down to the back room only once a year, on the winter solstice. The guide explained how the light strikes the left room, then passes to the center, then the right and in seventeen minutes flows back out the tunnel until the next year. Jenni got a bit claustrophobic on our way out the tunnel since we had to duck and twist to get through the stones. When we were out, Jenni told me she didn't like being squeezed like that to get out. So I asked her if she wanted me to explain what I thought Newgrange really was."

I glanced up to the other side of the table. Seven men had turned their full attention to me. All were silent, waiting. I decided to brave my own earthy explanation.

"The mound of Newgrange is the pregnant Earth, or the about to

become pregnant Earth. Once a year, at the winter solstice, the light beam of Father Sky penetrates Mother Earth. Starting in the left chamber, it highlights the esoteric symbols there, moves on to spark the sacred spiral in the central chamber, then as the Earth turns, radiates the right chamber with its stone eggs. Seventeen minutes after its entrance the wand of light recedes out the tunnel."

A glance around the table showed the men slightly stunned, open mouthed, in forward-leaning posture.

I pressed on. "I think druids held ceremonies inside to ensure the fertility of Earth, the crops, and the people. Once outside I told Jenni the reason she felt she was being squeezed was because she was being born again. Jenni looked back at the entrance of Newgrange, then back at me with a look of amazement."

I continued with a daring flourish, recounting what Jenni said to me.

" Yeaaah, right. Seventeen minutes, that's about right!"

The stunned silence erupted into a roar of laughter and talking. I thought, whew, that was close. Perhaps they had an added appreciation that we weren't prudish American ladies.

Then one of the men leaned toward me from across the table, "I've never heard that interpretation of Newgrange before. Wherever did you hear that?"

My cheeks grew warm, "After reading quite a bit about it, that is what made the most and obvious sense to me. You know, it seems kind of obvious." I said. What I failed to realize before I told the story was my interpretation of the meaning of Newgrange had never been heard by them before. It started off the dinner hour with lively conversation. I was quite pleased with myself.

Turin Castle on the far side of the ruins of the Rutherford estate.

CHAPTER XIX

TURIN CASTLE

The gravel road or grassy path we choose gives pace,
variety and direction to our journey,
as the tree-side bench, lost valley and green meadow
give the wild spaces and shadows of reverie
a momentary rest on the migration home.

~Leslie Lee, *Sacred Space*

Saturday 28 April
Delphi Lodge

LIZ HAD BEEN WAITING A LONG TIME for this day. We were to search for Turin Castle near Cong, adjacent to the home of Liz's husband's great-grandfather, a Rutherford, and for his grave. She had the name of the nearest town, Kilmaine, and the name of the seemingly hereditary caretakers of the manor, the Mooneys. The day was fine as we wound our way through the Partry Mountains to Leenane, along the isthmus between Lough Mask and Lough Corrib, to Cong, the home of enormous and storied Ashford Castle, built by the Norman de Burgos in the 1200s, and on to the backroads and byways of Kilmaine.

Down one rural road and up another, we felt we were circling Turin Castle but could not find it. Pulling up next to a farm truck with a man leaning

on it talking to someone inside, Josie lowered the window and when he sauntered up, she asked the slender, fair, fifty-year-old where Turin Castle might be. The exchange was so Irish. He smiled at her, tipped his head to the side to see the rest of us in the car, and comfortably leaned on the window frame as if we all had a thousand days to do nothing whatever, but enjoy the craic. Yes, yes, he could direct us, and why were we looking? At last we were off again after pulling forward to a wide spot in the road to turn around.

The sun was drifty, the fields passed slowly, a tractor driven by a lad approached on the side of the road toward us.

"Oh, my god, that's Jimmy driving that tractor!" In unison we all turned to stare.

Jimmy was Liz's second son, the one we saw a resemblance to in photos at our cousin's home just days before. He could be the twin of this passing farm boy. The recognition of familiar faces of those at home was once again happening in Ireland. But we pressed on for Turin Castle.

We pulled up along a stone fence. We saw the castle far across the field of the ruins of a house and outbuildings. It was a modest three or four story stone tower. That was all that was left of it, if there had ever been any more. Cool. After so long a search we were astounded to be there. Liz opened the gate, we drove into the yard, parked and piled out. Near the collapsed foundation of the house I pocketed a rock to give to Liz later as a gift.

The house was gone, but was marked by the marvelous ancient trees planted hundreds of years ago at the entrance.

Many native Irish have a negative attitude about trees that was difficult at first for me to understand. How could someone not love old trees? Why didn't the Irish plant trees where they'd gone missing? Why did they not revere these ancient, interesting species living in their midst? Where were the forests? The reasons are complex and heartbreaking. The brief explanation is they have no visual memory of ever having trees in their landscape. In their more recent history of the last eight hundred years, these old trees were planted on their ancestors' former lands by the invading Protestant English who took the land by force for their own landed gentry's ownership. It became a fad for the aristocrats to collect exotic tree species from around the world to plant on their beautiful Irish estates. It is understandably rancorous for the locals to see these huge pet

trees on the other side of tall stonewalls on vast, empty estates that were once filled with their families working the land and fishing its once public streams.

To the visitor, the huge, old specimen ancient oaks, yews, ash, fir, cedars of Lebanon, and even coast redwood, are all marvels. With its mild, moist climate, it seems almost any tree will grow in Ireland. Beyond the memories of any living Irish, history tells of the dense, deep forests that once covered much of Ireland. Indeed, trees, sacred groves, and the belief that all things were imbued with a god or spirit were integral to the druidic, pre-Christian Irish. The Irish alphabet, Ogham, is based on each letter represented by a tree and a portion of the year, with a special name and date for a tree of power, the *Bile Buadha*, on the 31st October. The Bile Buadha was planted in a sacred area outside the rath, or ringfort, of a king. This era, followed by the early Christian era, was a time when Ireland was revered as the center of the learned in Europe.

This rich, lovely land on the western edge of the world was, however, invaded and carved up time and time again. That happened first by a series of early legendary powers, then, Vikings, Normans, and English. With each successive rout, they were left with fewer forests. The Irish yew trees were cut for English long bows, and oaks for the English navy. In all of Ireland only a few hundred acres of native old growth forest remains.

The final blow of the hammer that completed the concussion that produced the amnesia of the trees was the 1840s potato famine crisis. The English landlords, across Ireland, forced hundreds of thousands of Irish off the lands they worked for rents on the English estates. This plunged them into extreme poverty, homelessness, and emigration. Some landowners were better to the locals than others, but cruelty seems to have been a national trend, and it left many native Irish with smoldering resentment and distrust toward the English on their great estates with their ancient trees. I think about this when I'm drawn to stand under the thick boughs and touch the bark on the trunk of a great old tree at an estate or castle.

This day in the countryside we met many charming and kind people. The Rutherfords, Liz explained, were an important Scottish family, and so we assumed the estate had been part of the English bestowal of Irish lands to the peerage. But in an interesting twist, this uncle left his family behind for the gold

rush in Australia. There he made his own fortune and settled in Ireland with his beloved stable of horses at the manor house at Turin Castle.

In search of the family gravesite of Liz's husband's family, we stopped in the local pub to ask about the cemetery. The proprietor, Mr. Welch, dropped his head, and shook it sadly saying that the cemetery where the Rutherfords were buried was in a terrible state of abandonment. He would take us there straightaway as it was close. We clambered over piles of bricks and stone and clots of earth. Weeds and stinging nettles had overgrown every recognizable thing. We gamely pulled aside shrubs from headstones until we found the Rutherford marker. Mr. Welch verbalized his feelings of regret that no one had cared for it as the relatives of all these people were gone, but that they would find someone who would put it to right. I could see he was pained to know what it would feel like to have traveled a great distance to pay respects to the ancestors only to find that no one had remembered them.

He hung his head while he murmured that this had been the protestant cemetery, and he was very sorry, but none were left. Ahhhh, I see. And I could see he felt that was no excuse. Another kindly man.

A beautiful Catholic cemetery.

Back at his pub in Kilmaine, Josie had a Guinness, we refreshed, traded addresses, and wrote down directions he explained to us for finding Michael Mooney. Michael was the last person who cared for the property and horses for the Rutherfords. After circling Turin Castle and the house and grounds looking for the address, we pulled into the drive of Mr. Mooney. We waited outside a few minutes before approaching the door. He walked slowly from the barn toward the car. I could see he had once been tall, with huge hands. From a distance, the typical Irish farmer looks quite well dressed. That includes a cap, shirt, dark vest, and wooly tweed jacket with practical pockets, pants tucked into the top of his tall rubber boots. Michael Mooney appeared well dressed, yet up close he was stooped with age and work, his face and hands creased, hardened, and worn. He had kind grey eyes and a patient way that was sure to be good with horses. He gently and quietly greeted each of us. Then we all climbed in the car to ride along so he could give us a personal tour of the grounds of the former Rutherford estate. After, we thanked him warmly, leaving him a small gift, exchanged addresses, and were on our way home.

Being charmed at the pub in Cong.

In Cong we stopped for a Guinness, aka, pit stop for Leslie where we met the prototypical charming Irishman. After only a few minutes of exchanging our narrative, he had somehow kissed all of us. Throughout all of this a young woman sat at the bar looking highly amused at the proceedings. I stepped up to pay the tab, said hello to the seated woman, and introduced the others and myself.

"You're his girlfriend, aren't you?" I asked.

"Yes, I am." She said with a smile.

Back at the lodge, showered, dressed, cocktail of choice entered into the booze book, I relaxed and conversed with the others in the library lounge before dinner. On our way in to be seated, the owner, Peter, escorted me to the head of the table for the dubious honor of having told a good story the previous night. Punishment it was, for they seated me next to a recent divorcee who was crying onto his plate for most of the dinner while I patted his hand that it would be all right and the others chatted about their day. No more stories from me!

In the remote Connemara Mountains in County Mayo.

Chapter XX

Spanish Bog People

Sunday 29 April
Delphi Lodge

What Were Those Children In The Road Doing? I thought after we'd passed them in the middle of the desolate Connemara mountains and bogs at the end of a long day of touring. In the rearview mirror, they appeared to be crouched at the edge of the road scraping gravel, or something, into piles with…a paper plate?

Two hundred yards later as I pulled over to make a U-turn, out loud, I asked, "What were those two children back there in the road doing?"

"I don't know. What happened?"

Backtracking, I pulled in the gravel wide spot where the children had been. There, pointing at the mountain, a minivan was front-end deep in muck up to the bumper.

The admonishment sprang to mind, *in a bog, do not step off the path.* It seems the driver had driven a bit too far off the parking area, over a hump, and into the bog. The children were collecting gravel to put under the tires. The mother was behind the steering wheel, father was knee-deep in bog trying to lift the front end of the vehicle. The system wasn't working.

"Hi, do you need some help?"

"No hablo Ingles."

"Liz! You're needed!"

How handy to have a Spanish-speaking sister. They conversed. Yes, it was indeed as we thought. We all headed down into the bog to join the father.

"One! Two! Three! Push!"

No go. His wife didn't know that rocking the car helps. We needed help.

"Jenni, see if you can herd a car over this way."

So Jenni stood in the middle of the road waiting as the sun set behind the mountain. Since no cars had passed us going either way for hours on this remote stretch of road, we knew it might be a long wait. But to our amazement in a few minutes a small Volkswagon car came along. Jenni stood in front of the car waving her arms overhead in universal semaphore. The driver stopped and Jenni approached the window to explain the situation. The car pulled to the side. Doors opened. Out clambered four huge guys. *Yay!*

I went to the driver side door of the stuck van and motioned the mother out of the car, got in, put it in reverse and with a few rocking motions, the guys had the van out in no time. We gave many thanks to the VW men, had much back and forth between Liz and the Spaniards, waved all around, and we followed the family until we parted ways.

It was a fortuitous ending to an excellent day of hiking in the mountains. Tonight, it was Liz's turn to tell the tale of the Spanish Bog People at dinner. I'd learned my lesson.

Monday 30 April
From Delphi Lodge, County Mayo
To Moy House, Lahinch, Co. Clare

We're sad to be nearing the end of our trip and to leave Delphi Lodge. In one short week we've traversed a country, come to love the people, and are going home with a thousand moments of camaraderie. Josie loved getting to know Jenni and Liz up close. She enjoyed the quirky continuity of seeing me appear to be reading stories to the sheep, cows, fish, trees and all as I sketched throughout the journey. Josie and I marveled at Liz and Jenni's ability to approach any stranger with aplomb. Josie delighted in the fish the way Liz delighted in getting to know the names and careers of the other guests at the Delphi Lodge. Years after the trip Josie still raved on about the taste of the local Guinness.

For Liz, it was about human connection: meeting people, finding out

about them, and fitting them into her collection, past, present, and future. That and the sense of being home struck Liz the most.

At home, Jenni best remembered the pony trekking, cattle herding, and exploring the beautiful Irish territory on foot.

While I love nothing more than to go exploring with a full tank of gas with a great group of friends, better yet, sisters, the parts of our trip that stayed with me most were my delight in the character and culture of the Irish people, the music, and the feeling of being home. All four of us experienced the sheer joy of simply being together.

Goodbyes all around at Delphi Lodge. We thunked our suitcases down the stairs, placed our tip money in the jar at the back door, and packed the trunk amid the trees and fly poles. We didn't let the dogs follow us.

By 10 a.m. we were finally off for the Burren. Recounting some of the funny moments of the trip, we remembered when Jenni imbibed one tiny thimbleful of champagne together in our rooms before heading down to dinner. As we waited for her outside the bathroom we heard a gargling scream. We turned to look. Thinking she had picked up the small complimentary mouthwash, she had instead drained the shampoo. One too many drinks for her.

Jenni's (really Josie's) Words of the Day:
Liz, disappointed, said, "I've used up all my bath suds."
To which Josie quipped, "Yeah, too bad Jenni drank hers."

BallyVaughn

Chapter XXI

The Spirit of Ireland

What is a door but a threshold of mystery
to close against the storm or open to the wind—
to bar the dragonflies of maps and compass box
that land within the rucksack of the youthful mind,
or open to the pilgrim seeking sanctuary.

~Leslie Lee, *Sacred Space*

Monday 30 April
Delphi Lodge to Moy House

It Feels Good To Have Been Here long enough to have stopped again at O'Brien's Pub in Ballyvaughn for lunch. We took the beautiful coast road south to Moy House. We were all quite tired and looking forward to a day close to home. We arrived at 5 p.m. It's not just having started the trip at Moy House, it's that I love this place, and am feeling at home.

It's Beltine meaning *light-fire*, the Celtic May Day, beginning tonight as is the Irish custom of starting a holiday at eve the night before. Beltine marks the quarter festival between the Spring Equinox and the Summer Solstice. In the early days on mountaintops and in town centers across all of Ireland, people lit bonfires this night, and danced, performed fertility rituals, and prepared for open grazing of the cows throughout the following day.

147

Tuesday 1 May
Moy House, Lahinch, County Clare

I'll miss the quintessential Irish breakfasts. Fresh linens are laid under matching floral china surrounded by gleaming utensils, vases of flowers, populated with baskets of croissants, butter bowls, yogurt parfaits, and jams. The teapot, piping hot, takes center stage while it steeps the golden brown tea. Cream floats in the matching china creamer and sugar lumps fill the bowl. In this cool, damp climate, the Irish warm the plates and preheat the pots. Every course, no matter how humble the abode, is changed out with sets of fresh place-settings. It's a pleasure even before the breakfast arrives. The food itself deserves special mention: flatback bacon baked brown with slightly curling edges, black rings of blood sausage, eggs how you like them, room temperature brown bread toast in a caddy, crispy wafers of potato cakes, sprigs of parsley, and the juice of one's choice.

This morning after breakfast we hung chestnut tree sprigs of new growth on our doors for Bealtine.

We walked the beach, and lunched in Lahinch. Jenni had seen the sign about pony trekking, "Try it! You'll like it!" She went off to ride while the rest of us napped, packed, and I colored in some artwork. She came back relating how the horse owner was also an official matchmaker. At one point she asked him how many horses he had. He said he didn't know. "He didn't believe in counting them."

Dinner at Moy House was excellent. We enjoyed the company of a charming couple staying there.

We were all off to O'Connor's Pub in Doolin for music. How I love this unofficial capitol of traditional music in Ireland, even with the tour buses flowing past for the Aran Islands tour, and the tourists packing in. Tables are tucked here and there around corners and in tiny rooms, but mostly ranged around a U-shaped booth with a sign over it stating it was reserved for the musicians. The bar is peppered with emblems from police and fire departments from around the world stapled to the walls. Wooden surfaces are simple and worn.

Christy Berry and Michael Kelleher at O'Connor's Pub in Doolin.

We arrived early enough to choose a prime table across from the musicians so I could draw. The place packed in, drinks plunked down. A man with a fiddle scooted in around the table, then a man with a concertina-squeeze box, then a flutist, an Irish whistler, a drummer with a bodhran.

Without ceremony they began to play for each other. Their eyes were constantly flicking to one another to check the pace or changes. They were not playing to the audience. They were not on a platform. They had no amplification. They had a beer in front of them and they had the music of the others.

People crowded in around us squeezed into every niche, leaning on me, then peering down to see that I was drawing and watching the images appear before their eyes. Christy Berry, Michael Kelleher, Patrick, Colin Nea. Chairs pulled up for newcomers who followed the signal of an unseen lead. I crouched over my painting with my glass of gin, paintbrush, and pen in the dark, jostled, loving it. I wished the pub scene at home was as intimate as this.

Christy Berry, Michael Kelleher, Colin Nea, and fellow musicians, Thomas, and Dave.

Colin Nea, Christy Berry's hands, and Patrick on the violin.

Chapter XXII

The Circle Closes

*The moments perish as I write, yet still I wish
these salted stones and amber wood, in service to
the heart of goodness, last a thousand years for those
who stay and strive to make the world a better place;
or should we fail, these words inspire another hope.*

~Leslie Lee, *Sacred Space*

*Wednesday 2 May
Depart from Shannon Airport, Ireland
To Traverse City, Michigan USA*

It Is Sad To Leave. Perhaps with some of our connections we can find one or two wonderful places to stay that are affordable for a long visit. We all loved Lahinch, but it's to the Dingle Peninsula, West Cork, the Connemara, and County Mayo that I would like to explore more for the mountains, lakes, wildness, and cliffy shores. We had another beautiful day for our flight out. I felt all the cells of my body ache to return to Ireland, the land of my origins. I thought, *thank you, thank you, thank you.*

At breakfast, Liz, Jenni, and Josie presented me with a box, a gift. I opened it. It was a lovely piece of pale blue beach glass welded to a bracelet top. I looked at them. "Awww, you guys, thank you, I love it."

I turned it over. Engraved on the back it said, "Go raibh maith agat."

In Irish, *Thank you.*

Thursday 3 May
Elk Rapids, Michigan

Here I sit in my yellow chair from which I planned the trip to Ireland and read my books, and took my notes, and tried to saturate my being with the place vicariously. I'm back after five weeks, sitting here, searching for the words to express the experience. The traumatic departure from my own home and family of my childhood shaped my life in ever resolving themes of home and acceptance. Traveling to the old country with my sisters was like dropping anchor in homeport after years at sea.

It is almost without exception, the great talent of the Irish people to be hospitable without seeming servile in the least. Each person makes a personal connection even if just for a moment and now having been there in the midst of it, those thousand subtle connections, I can see how in America we race and skim over the tops of each other in our everyday life not pausing to allow the time to directly connect. I imagine for the Irish visiting here it would seem quite rude to be bumped about in our abrupt exchanges as if no one mattered. They would fail to understand the point, the goal, the ring of success, without having enjoyed and lived through the experience of getting there. I think of the Irish as being the most welcoming people I've ever met, yet candid and totally unabashed about speaking their minds.

Ireland has an incredibly democratic society, whether more money or less, or family structure higher or lower, or more or less educated. You can sense it. They feel they have a simple right to their own opinion, to own the land they stand on, and to be treated with the dignity of being human. It allows for greater freedom of expression even if others don't agree. Just that it is accepted to be oneself. I think we Americans must appear quite guarded and formulated to the Irish and perhaps always wishing to be someone other than who we really are. They are generous of spirit.

The point, the goal, the ring of success, without having enjoyed and lived through the experience of getting there. Anyway, I think of the Irish as being the most hospitable I've ever met, yet candid and totally unabashed about speaking their minds. On the whole, an incredibly democratic society — each person, whether more money or less, or family stature higher or lower, or more or less educated — all, you can sense it, feel they have a simple right to their own opinion and to be treated with the dignity of being human. It allows for greater freedom of expression — not that others won't disagree! just that is accepted to be oneself. I think we Americans must appear quite guarded and formulated to the Irish, and perhaps always wishing to be someone other than who we really are.

They are generous of spirit.

Last excerpt from my travel journal written at home.

ACKNOWLEDGMENTS

Having reached that certain age when it makes sense to do only the things that are important to me, I've decided to share parts of my life. This surprises me, since as an introvert, I've thus far guarded against it. It is with the help of many others that I'm able to express myself in print. Foremost I'm reliant on my co-worker of fifteen years, Byrdie Butka. She handles the everyday details of my life at the office now that I travel, study, write, and paint. Invariably warm and loving, Byrdie's kindly exterior sheaths an extraordinary intelligence and ability that seems to fill every need.

The travel writing project has been a major undertaking. This one book, *We Are the Land: Ireland*, is the first in a series of thirty years of traveling with my journals and paint box. Five years ago, I had stacks of dog-eared, rained upon, battered original journals. Mary Meredith, office maven, typed the verbatim texts following my tiny handwriting, arrows, varying sized books for the same trip, slips of paper inserts, food and wine smears, and torn pages.

The Old Town Writer's Group has sustained me and moved my work forward twice a month for the last six years. Their guidance has made me a better writer, and their friendship has brought me out of the den in which writer's dwell. By serendipity, Samantha Fisher breezed in from Australia to join the group. She brought her refreshing youth and poetry home before her next foray across the globe. We talked travel writing, and I engaged her services to help me set up a system for digitizing my illustrations. Scott Wilson, owner of Vada Color, expertly photographed and printed the art resulting in these gorgeous re-productions. The complexity of organizing and tracking on nearly two thousand images created over three decades almost did us in. Almost. Samantha escaped on her travels and returned a year later. Between trips, she rejoined the writer's group and this project to handle all manner of details—typing the bibliography and reading list chief among them.

A special thank you to friends Susie Galbraith, Patrick Harrington, and Lillian Randall for regularly allowing me to torture them with early versions over

a glass of Irish whisky. Friends and colleagues in writing and freshwater topics, Jerry and Gail Dennis, introduced me to other writing professionals in the area, notably former Managing Editor of the *Detroit News*, Jennifer Carroll. A whirl-wind of positive energy and expertise, Jennifer edited *We Are the Land: Ireland*. She helped transform my writing from the realm of the personal to a world in which readers could share and professionals would respect. Gail Dennis and I then sat side-by-side working on the stunning layout of the book. Her unfailing sense of beauty and proportion has helped create this visual feast. Not to mention that she had to tame the computer to make it happen. Thank you to those invisible helpers at Jenkins Group, especially Yvonne Roehler who waved her magic wand and sprinkled the book with professional fairy dust.

To my advance readers Thomas Lynch, Jerry Dennis, George and Vivienne Nixon, and Diana Beresford-Kroeger whose thoughts and hearts I trust, and to all who helped this book become real, as they say in Ireland, "Go raibh mile maith agat." A thousand thank yous.

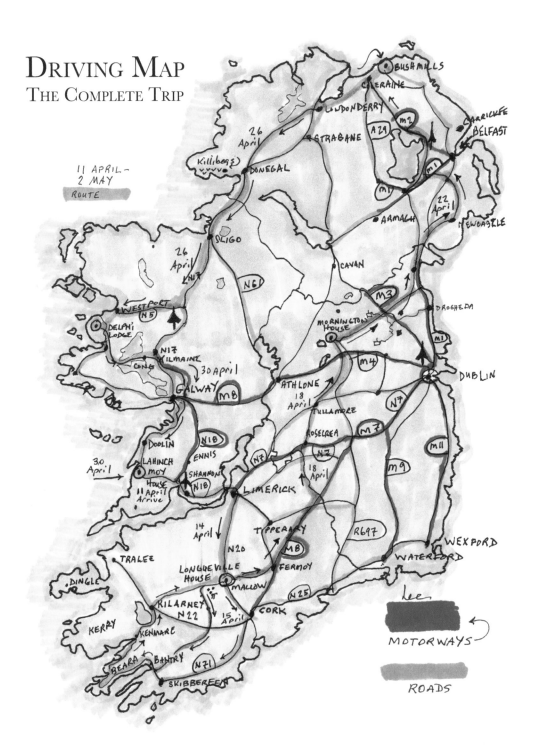

Driving Map
The Complete Trip

11 APRIL –
2 MAY
ROUTE

BUSHMILLS
COLERAINE
LONDONDERRY
CARRICKFE BELFAST
STRABANE
A 29
M2
26
April
Killibegs
DONEGAL
M1
22
April
ARMAGH
NEWCASTLE
26
April
N17
SLIGO
CAVAN
N61
M3
DROGHEDA
WESTPORT
N5
MORNINGTON
HOUSE
M1
DELPHI
LODGE
N17
KILMAINE
30 April
CONG
M4
DUBLIN
GALWAY
M8
ATHLONE
18
April
N7
TULLAMORE
DOOLIN
N18
ENNIS
ROSCREA
M7
m11
LAHINCH
MOY
N7
N7
m9
3,0
April
SHANNON
N18
HOUSE
11 April
Arrive
LIMERICK
18
April
WEXFORD
TIPPERARY
R697
14
April
N20
M8
WATERFORD
TRALEE
LONGUEVILLE
HOUSE
FERMOY
DINGLE
MALLOW
N25
KILLARNEY
N22
15
April
CORK
KERRY
KENMARE
Lee
MOTORWAYS
BEARA
BANTRY
N71
SKIBBEREEN
ROADS

ILLUSTRATION DETAILS TO ORDER PRINTS

2007 3 31	Ireland, Co. Clare, Doolin, O'Connor's Pub, Amy Williams, Christy Barry, Michael Kelleher, John Williams
2007 4 12	Ireland, Co. Clare, Cliffs of Moher
2007 4 13	Ireland, Co. Clare, 1. At Cooney's in Quilty 2. At the Atlantic Hotel
2007 4 13	Ireland, Co. Clare, Loophead Peninsula
2007 4 14	Ireland, Co. Cork. Mallow, Longueville House, Fireplace Mount
2007 4 14	Ireland, Co. Cork, Mallow, Longueville House, Josie and Jenni at Dinner
2007 4 15	Ireland, Co. Cork, Glouthane, Standing Stone
2007 4 15	Ireland, Co. Cork, Glouthane, 1. Standing Stone in Distance 2. Glouthane Stone and Dolman
2007 4 16	Ireland, Co. Kerry, Killarney, Speakeasy Pub, Ladbroke's Jacket
2007 4 17	Ireland, Co. Cork, Mallow, Longueville House, Front Door
2007 4 18	Ireland, Co. Laois, Abbeyleix, At Morrisey's
2007 4 18	Ireland, Driving Map, April 18
2007 4 19	Ireland, Co. Meath, Knowth, NW Stone
2007 4 19	Ireland, Co. Meath, Knowth, 1. Standing Stone at The Entry 2. Curbstone Etched
2007 4 19	Ireland, Co. Meath, Knowth, 1. Entrance with Pool 2. Newgrange Profile
2007 4 19	Ireland, Co. Meath, Newgrange, Entrance
2007 4 19	Ireland, Co. Meath, Newgrange, 1. Left Basin 2. Central Basin
2007 4 19	Ireland, Co. Meath, Newgrange, Right Basin
2007 4 19	Ireland, Co. Meath, Hill Of Tara, Lia Fail
2007 4 19	Ireland, Co. Meath, Hill of Tara, Two Hawthorns
2007 4 19	Ireland, Co. Meath, Trim Castle
2007 4 20	Ireland, Co. Westmeath, Mornington House, Ann and Liz
2007 4 23	Ireland, Dublin, Harry's Bar Taps
2007 4 24	Ireland, Co. Down, Castlewellen, Lamps in the Restaurant
2007 4 24	Ireland, Co. Antrim, Bushmills Inn Fireplace
2007 4 24	Ireland, Co, Antrim, Portrush, A Guinness

2007 4 26   Ireland, Co. Mayo, Delphi Lodge, Front Door
2007 4 26   Ireland, Co. Mayo, Delphi Lodge, Annual Salmon Release
2007 4 28   Ireland, Co. Mayo, Turin Castle
2007 5 1   Ireland, Co. Clare, Doolin, O'Connor's Pub, Christy Barry,
             and Michael Kelleher
2007 5 1   Ireland, Co. Clare, Doolin, O'Connor's Pub,
             1. Christy Barry's Hand
             2. Patrick on Violin
2007 5 1   Ireland, Co. Clare, Doolin, O'Connor's Pub,
             1. Colin Nea, The Legend
             2. Christy Barry on Spoons and Bodhran
2007 5 3   Michigan, Elk Rapids, Swan at Home

To order prints of illustrations, maps, and charts,
please go to my web site LeeStudioTC.com,
or ask your local bookstore to kindly carry them.
Refer to the titles used on these pages
starting with the date when you order. Thank you.

MAP AND CHART DETAILS TO ORDER PRINTS

2007 4 11	Ireland, Driving Map, Full Route, April 11 Through May 2
2007 4 11	Ireland, Driving Map, April 11
2007 4 11	Ireland, Driving Map, April 11 Close Up
2007 4 11	Ireland, Road Map, Old Roads
2007 4 11	Ireland, Road Map, Old Roads, Color
2007 4 11	Ireland, Road Map, Driving Times and Tips
2007 4 11	Ireland, Map, Counties of Ireland
2007 4 11	Ireland, Map, Provinces of Ireland
2007 4 11	Ireland, Map, Boyne River Valley Megaliths
2007 4 11	Ireland, Map, The Steppes
2007 4 11	Ireland, Timeline of Prehistory, 60,000 ya – 10,000 ya
2007 4 11	Ireland, Timeline of Prehistory, 10,000 ya – 7,000 ya
2007 4 11	Ireland, Timeline of Prehistory, 7,000 ya – 4,000 ya
2007 4 11	Ireland, Timeline of Prehistory, 4,000 ya – 1,000 ya
2007 4 11	Tomb Types
2007 4 11	Irish DNA
2007 4 14	Ireland, Driving Map, April 14
2007 4 14	Ireland, Driving Map, April 14 Close Up
2007 4 15	Ireland, Driving Map, April 15 Close Up
2007 4 18	Ireland, Driving Map, April 18
2007 4 22	Ireland, Driving Map, April 22
2007 4 22	Ireland, Driving Map, April 22 Close Up
2007 4 26	Ireland, Driving Map, April 26 Close Up

PRONUNCIATION OF MODERN IRISH

Excerpted from James MacKillop's Oxford Dictionary of Celtic Mythology.

a	f<u>a</u>ther
á	l<u>a</u>w
e	<u>e</u>nd
é	c<u>a</u>me
i	<u>i</u>t
í	<u>ea</u>ch
o	p<u>u</u>ll (Note from author: Old Irish was o as in <u>o</u>dd)
ó	ode
u	p<u>u</u>ll
ú	spoon

P-celtic split from Q-celtic approximately three thousand years ago.
Gaulish, Welsh, Cornish and Breton (Brythonic) as in the time of Caesar's Britain.
Q-celtic (goidelic)
Irish, Scottish, Gaelic, Manx
In Irish, Q-celtic head is caenn. In Welsh, head is pen.

bh	before or after a or u:	<u>w</u>alrus
bh	before or after e or i:	sli<u>v</u>er
c	before or after consonants:	<u>c</u>limate
ch	before or after a or u:	Ba<u>ch</u> or lo<u>ch</u>
ch	before or after e or i:	<u>h</u>it
d	like dh	
dh	before and after a and o:	ro<u>g</u>o (Spanish)
dh	before and after e or i:	y (English)
fh:	silent	
gh	before and after a and o:	ro<u>g</u>o
gh	before and after e or i:	English y
mh	before and after a or o:	<u>w</u>alrus
mh	before and after e or i:	sli<u>v</u>er
s	before and after a or o:	<u>s</u>ong
s	before and after e or i:	<u>sh</u>ip
sh:	<u>h</u>ope	
T	before and after a or o:	<u>th</u>ought
t	before and after e or i:	<u>t</u>une (British)
th:	<u>h</u>ope	

Reading List and Bibliography

Allentoft, M. E., et al. "Population Genomics of Bronze Age Eurasia." *Nature International Journal of Science.* (June 11, 2015.) https://www.nature.com/articles/nature14507

Anthony, David W. *The Horse, The Wheel, and Language: How Bronze-Age Riders from the Eurasian Steppes Shaped the Modern World.* Princeton University Press, 2007.

Ascherson, Neal. *Black Sea.* Hill and Wang, 1995.

Barry, Terry, ed. *A History of Settlement in Ireland.* Taylor & Francis, 2002

Bell, Jonathan, and Mervyn Watson. *A History of Irish Farming, 1750-1950.* Four Courts Press, 2008.

Boylan, Henry. *A Dictionary of Irish Biography.* Gill & Macmillan, 1999.

Brennan, Martin. *The Stones of Time: Calendars, Sundials, and Stone Chambers of Ancient Ireland.* Inner Traditions International, 1994.

Burl, Aubrey. *Prehistoric Astronomy and Ritual.* Shire Archaeology, 1983.

Burl, Aubrey. *Prehistoric Stone Circles.* 3rd ed. Shire Archaeology, 2001.

Byrne, Francis John. Irish Kings and High-Kings. 2nd ed., Four Courts Press, 2001.

Cahill, Thomas. *How The Irish Saved Civilization: The Untold Story of Ireland's Heroic Role from the Fall of Rome to the Rise of Medieval Europe.* Hodder and Stoughton, 2003.

Cassidy, Lara M., et al. "Neolithic and Bronze Age Migration to Ireland and Establishment of the Insular Atlantic Genome." *Proceedings of the National Academy of Sciences* 113, no. 2 (January 12, 2016.) http://www.pnas.org/content/113/2/368

Castleden, Rodney. *Britain 3000 BC.* Sutton, 2003.

Cavalli-Sforza, Luigi Luca, and Francesco Cavalli-Sforza. *The Great Human Diasporas: The History of Diversity and Evolution*. Translated by Sarah Thorne. Addison-Wesley Publishing Company, 1995.

Cavalli-Sforza, Luigi Luca. *Genes, Peoples, and Languages*. Translated by Mark Seielstad. North Point Press, 2006.

Collis, John. *The Celts: Origins, Myths, and Inventions*. Tempus Publishing, 2003.

Connolly, S.J., editor. *The Oxford Companion to Irish History*. 2nd ed., Oxford University Press, 2002.

Constable, Nick. *World Atlas of Archaeology*. London: Thalamus, 2009.

Cooney, Gabriel, and Eoin Grogan. *Irish Prehistory: A Social Perspective*. Wordwell, 1994.

Cunliffe, Barry W. *Europe Between The Oceans: Themes and Variations, 9000 BC-AD 1000*. Yale University Press, 2011.

Cunliffe, Barry W. *Facing the Ocean: The Atlantic and Its Peoples, 8000 BC-AD 1500*. Oxford University Press, 2001.

Cunliffe, Barry W. *The Oxford Illustrated History of Prehistoric Europe*. Oxford University Press, 2001.

Davies, Norman. *The Isles: A History*. Oxford University Press, 1999.

Dinneen, Patrick S. *Focloir Saeoilse Asus Bearla: An Irish-English Dictionary, Being a Thesaurus of the Words, Phrases and Idioms of the Modern Irish Language*. Published for the Irish Texts Society, by the Educational Co. of Ireland, 1996.

Dixon-Kennedy, Mike. *A Companion to Arthurian and Celtic Myths and Legends*. Sutton, 2004.

Duffy, Seán, et al. *Atlas of Irish History*, Dublin: Gill & Macmillan, 2000.

Ekwall, Eilert. *Oxford Dictionary of English Place-Names*. Clarendon Press, 1947.

Ellis, Peter Berresford. *A Brief History of the Druids*. Robinson, 2002.

Fagan, Brian. *The Long Summer: How Climate Changed Civilization*. Basic Books, 2004.

Flanagan, Deidre and Laurence. *Irish Place Names*. Gill & Macmillan, 2002.

Galvin, Stephen, D., "The Impact of Volcanic Eruptions on the Climate and Ecology of Ireland since A.D. 1800." *Department of Geography and Archaeology* at The National University of Ireland, Galway. (December 20, 2010.) https://aran.library.nuigalway.ie/bitstream/handle/10379/2021/Galvin Thesie.pdf?sequence=1&isAllowed=y

Guthrie, R. Dale. *The Nature of Paleolithic Art*. University of Chicago Press, 2005.

Haak, W., et al. "Massive Migration from the Steppe was a Source for Indo-European Languages in Europe." *Nature International Journal of Science*. (March 2, 2015.) https://www.ncbi.nlm.nih.gov/pmc/articles/PMC5048219/

Halpin, Andrew, and Conor Newman. *Ireland: An Oxford Archaeological Guide to Sites from Earliest Times to AD 1600*. Oxford University Press, 2006.

Harbison, Peter. *Pre-Christian Ireland: From The First Settlers to The Early Celts*. Thames and Hudson, 1988.

Heaney, Seamus. *District and Circle*. Faber and Faber, 2006.

Homann, Johann Baptist. *Hiberniae Regnum Ultoniae, Connaciae, Laceniae, Momoniae (Ireland.)* [original map.] Scale not given. Nuremberg, Germany: J.B. Homann, 1712.

Johnson, James. *The Scots and Scotch-Irish in America*. Lerner Publications, 1991.

Kearns, Hugh. *The Mysterious Chequered Lights of Newgrange*. Elo Publications, 1993.

Killeen, Richard. *A Timeline of Irish History*. Gill & Macmillan, 2003.

Lynch, Michael, ed. *The Oxford Companion to Scottish History*. Oxford University Press, 2001.

Lynch, Thomas. *Booking Passage: We Irish & Americans*. W. W. Norton & Company, 2005.

MacKillop, James. *Dictionary of Celtic Mythology*. Oxford University Press, 1998.

MacLysaght, Edward. *The Surnames of Ireland*. Irish Academic Press, 2005.

MacNeill, Máire. *The Festival of Lughnasa: A Study of the Survival of the Celtic Festival of the Beginning of Harvest*. Comhairle Bhéaloideas Éireann, 2008.

McCaffrey, Carmel, and Leo Eaton. *In Search of Ancient Ireland: The Origins of the Irish, from Neolithic Times to the Coming of the English*. New Amsterdam Books, 2002.

McCaffrey, Carmel. *In Search of Ireland's Heroes: The Story of the Irish from the English Invasion to the Present Day*. Ivan R. Dee, 2007.

McCourt, Malachy. *Malachy McCourt's History of Ireland*. Running Press Book Publishers, 2004.

McCullough, David W. *Wars of the Irish Kings: A Thousand Years of Struggle from the Age of Myth through the Reign of Queen Elizabeth I*. Three Rivers Press, 2002.

McDonnell, Hector. *Irish Round Towers*. Wooden, 2005.

McMann, Jean. *Loughcrew The Cairns: A Guide to an Ancient Irish Landscape*. After Hours Books, 2005.

Michelin Travel Publications, *Ireland* [map.] 1 cm : 4 km. Paris: Michelin, 2006.

Mitchell, Frank, and Michael Ryan. *Reading the Irish Landscape*. Town House, 2003.

Monaghan, Patricia. *The Encyclopedia of Celtic Mythology and Folklore*. Checkmark Books, 2008.

Moroney, Anne-Marie. *Dowth: Winter Sunsets*. Flax Mill Publications, 1999.

Mountfort, Paul Rhys. *Ogam, The Celtic Oracle of the Trees: Understanding, Casting, and Interpreting the Ancient Druidic Alphabet*. Destiny Books, 2002.

Myres, N. M., et al. "A Major Y-chromosome Haplogroup R1b Holocene Era Founder Effect in Central and Western Europe." *European Journal of Human Genetics*. (August 25, 2010.) http://www.nature.com/ejhg/journal/v19/n1/full/ejhg2010146a.html?message=remove

O'Donoghue, Jo, and Seán McMahon. *Brewer's Dictionary of Irish Phrase and Fable*. Weidenfeld & Nicolson, 2004.

Ó hÓgáin, Dáithí. *The Lore of Ireland: An Encyclopaedia of Myth, Legend and Romance*. Collins Press, 2006.

Oppenheimer, Stephen. *Origins of The British: A Genetic Detective Story: The Surprising Roots of the English, Irish, Scottish, and Welsh*. Carroll & Graf Publishers, 2006.

Pennick, Nigel. *Celtic Sacred Landscapes*. Thames & Hudson, 2000.

Quinn, Bob. *The Atlantean Irish: Ireland's Oriental and Maritime Heritage*. Lilliput Press, 2005.

Raftery, Barry. *Pagan Celtic Ireland: The Enigma of the Irish Iron Age*. Thames & Hudson, 1994.

Reich, David. *Who We Are and How We Got Here: Ancient DNA and the New Science of the Human Past*. Pantheon Books, 2018.

Rosenberg, Donna. *World Mythology: An Anthology of the Great Myths and Epics*. 2nd ed., National Textbook Co., 1994.

Rudgley, Richard. *The Lost Civilizations of the Stone Age*. Touchstone, 2000.

Ryan, William, and Walter Pitman. *Noah's Flood: The New Scientific Discoveries About the Event That Changed History*. Simon & Schuster, 1998.

Scarre, Chris. *Smithsonian Timelines of the Ancient World*. Dorling Kindersley, 1993.

Schama, Simon. *A History of Britain: The Wars of the British 1603-1776*. Vol. 2. 3 vols. Hyperion, 2001.

Shepherd, William R. *Shepherd's Historical Atlas*. 9th ed. New York: Barnes & Noble, 1964.

Smyth, William J. *Map-making, Landscapes and Memory: Colonial and Early Modern Ireland C.1530-1750*. Cork University Press in Association with Field Day, 2006.

Squire, Charles. *Celtic Myth & Legend, Poetry & Romance*. Bell Publishing, 1979.

Stafford, Pauline. *Unification and Conquest: A Political and Social History of England in the Tenth and Eleventh Centuries*. Edward Arnold, 1989.

Stanley, Steven M. *Children of the Ice Age: How a Global Catastrophe Allowed Humans to Evolve*. W.H. Freeman and Company, 1998.

Sykes, Bryan. *Adams Curse: A Future Without Men*. Corgi, 2010.

Sykes, Bryan. *Saxons, Vikings, and Celts: The Genetic Roots of Britain and Ireland*. W. W. Norton & Company, 2006.

Sykes, Bryan. *The Seven Daughters of Eve: The Science That Reveals Our Genetic Ancestry*. W. W. Norton & Company, 2001.

Thomas, N. L. *Irish Symbols of 3500 BC*. Mercier Press, 1988.

Tilley, Christopher. *Metaphor and Material Culture*. Blackwell, 1999.

Tillinghast, Richard. *Finding Ireland: A Poet's Explorations of Irish Literature and Culture*. University of Notre Dame Press, 2008.

Trager, James. *The Peoples Chronology: A Year-by-Year Record of Human Events from Prehistory to the Present*. Henry Holt and Company, 1994.

Uistín, Liam Mac. *Exploring Newgrange*. O'Brien Press, 1999.

Waddell, John. *The Prehistoric Archaeology of Ireland*. Wordwell, 2000.

Wade, Nicholas. *Before the Dawn: Recovering the Lost History of Our Ancestors*. Penguin, 2006.

Wells, Spencer. *The Journey of Man: A Genetic Odyssey*. Random House, 2002.

Wright, Dennis M. "A set of Distinctive Marker Values Defines a Y-STR Signature for Gaelic Dalcassian Families." *Journal of Genetic Genealogy*. (January 4, 1999.) https://www.academia.edu/9125818/A_set_of_ Distinctive_Marker_Values_Defines_a_Y-STR_Signature_for_Gaelic_ Dalcassian_Families

Yeats, William Butler. *The Collected Poems of William Butler Yeats*. Macmillan, 1955.

Zaczek, Iain. *Chronicles of the Celts*. Sterling Publishing, 1997.

Zucchelli, Christine. *Stones of Adoration: Sacred Stones and Mystic Megaliths of Ireland*. Collins Press, 2007.

Travel List for Ireland

Items to Pack:

Passport
Medications
Money, foreign currency, credit cards
Phone and charger, plus extra charger
Computer, Kindle, iPad
Earphones
Books, puzzles, Sudoku
Sunglasses, glasses
Calendar and contacts, in print
Itinerary
Art supplies
Gifts
Pin number, travel numbers for airlines
Fan
Maps and GPS
Instant coffee
Earplugs
Toothbrush and toiletries
Sewing kit
Ziploc bags, zip ties
Solar, hand generator
Water purification system
Lightweight daypack
Laundry soap
Folding cup
Copies of credit cards and passport in a
secure location

International or domestic
carry-on size suitcase with
four wheels
Half size four-wheeled briefcase as personal carry-on

Essential Clothes:

Rain coat, long or 3/4 length
Rain jacket with rain pants
Featherweight anorak or
wind jacket
Evening shoes, evening dress
Jewelry
Slippers
Light waterproof boots
Water sandals
Boots, black for town
Walking shoes
Bathing suit
Pajamas
Billed cap, knit cap, gloves,
Midge net with brimmed hat
Scarves, shawls
Socks
Pants
Shirts

TRAVEL PACKING FOR IRELAND

Midge nets:

In Ireland and Scotland midges are not big floppy freshwater hatches of fish food, but clouds of tiny biting insects that love the carbon dioxide from your breath, and the moisture from your eyes and ears. If you're going out in the countryside and you don't know if it's midge season, stuff a midge net in your pocket to unroll over the brim of your hat just to be sure. Make sure the net has small enough holes to keep those tiny guys out. I've not experienced them in Ireland, but I take my net anyway.

Raincoats and waterproof boots:

My traveling companion, Byrdie, bought the cutest raincoat ever to take to Scotland. On our first day of rain she wore it out into the fields to visit a stone circle. It rained right through the polka dots. She was wet, cold, and miserable. Either take a real raincoat, at least two-thirds length, with a hood that has a drawstring and brim or buy one immediately when you arrive. If you plan to hike or visit the islands, take waterproof pants as well. I love sitting outside on deck in the wind and rain knowing I'll be toasty warm and dry even if the interior seating is full. Boots for hiking or hill walking should be lightweight and waterproof. I always take a flyweight anorak folded into its pocket in my daypack or purse.

Gifts:

Ideal gifts are authentic items from home that are lightweight enough to pack. If not a poem, song, or dance to share, then I take scarves, Petoskey stones, aprons with cherries printed on them (my home is the cherry capital), dried cherries, and CDs of early jazz and blues artists. At one country house hotel, I left an apron to be given to the chef with apologies for its feminine design the night before we left. The next morning the breakfast room was atwitter. The server told me as I sat at our table that the chef loved the gift and wrote me a thank-you note. It was a paper folded on my plate. I flipped it open to discover a photo printed on it of the quite hairy chef wearing only the cherry covered apron without a stitch

on underneath, arms spread wide in thanks and a huge smile. "I love the apron, sorry I'm not a lady chef." We all had a terrific laugh.

Medications:
Take your usual prescription meds with a copy of the prescription, as well as at least a few of any over-the-counter medications you might need under a variety of circumstances. Pack a decent first aid kit. Include moleskin and blister bandages. Liquid medicines may be taken away at customs, so try to take only dry medicine. I carry Polysporin to keep my nostrils moist and antibacterial lotion with me in all group settings, especially the airplane.

Clothes:
Take colorful silk scarves to jazz up the usual black, brown, or blue pants and shirts. Silk packs incredibly lightly and can be washed in the sink and dried on a towel or hanger.

Jewelry:
Take fun, inexpensive pieces that you don't mind losing, and won't target you to predators.

Documents and credit cards:
Keep copies where you can access them and others can't. Memorize pin numbers.

Toiletries:
Among the usual, take a small bar of soap and a washcloth just in case you stay in the barest of accommodations. I take several small bottles of shampoos and lotions. As one is used I toss it away making room as I go. Take quart and gallon size Ziplock bags. Take your favorite clothes washing granules. In Europe, I wash most of my clothes by hand in the sink or tub, squeeze out the water, roll the clothes in a towel, stand on that to absorb the excess, then hang items out or drape them on the warming heaters.

Extras:

These items don't take much room, but might save the day: zip ties in several sizes (keep them in an outer pocket to secure your bag's zipper if needed,) fish line, a small roll of duct tape, tiny flashlights that clip to the suitcase, a folding knife with scissors and wine opener (pack in checked luggage), extra cords for electronics, a solar or hand charger, Ziplock bags for everything from muddy boots to the days lunch. I take Tyvek mailers to ship gifts or extra clothes home, and break the packing tape from the dispenser, step on it, and stuff it in the corner of my suitcase. Do not pack batteries in stowed luggage. Carry them on.

Packing Cubes:

Buy super lightweight, zippered nylon boxes of different colors for all of your clothes. Pants fit in one larger size, shirts have a special folding version, underwear, tank tops, scarves, and pajamas have their own cubes. When you open your suitcase, or if U.S. Customs officials do, you'll be happy to have everything neat and in its place. It's a snap to unpack and repack. Just place the cubes in the drawers or on shelves and you're done. I take one of those superlight zippered small duffle bags or daypack that folds up. When I arrive, all my outerwear goes into that and onto the back seat or trunk.

Suitcase:

Lighten up! A great, lightweight suitcase with four wheels that fully-packed weighs only twenty-five to thirty-five pounds is perfect for lifting into overhead bins and dragging up the stairs. Try for an international carry-on or the slightly larger domestic carry-on. Or buy a high quality backpack with wheels of the same size. For my personal carry-on I use a small half rolling briefcase packed with one overnight's essentials, plus whatever I want on board, and all my valuables. I leave enough room for a smaller purse to go inside it.

IRISH PLACE NAMES

Please see Deidre and Laurence Flanagan, *Irish Place Names.*

abh – river
achadh – field
ard or aird – hill, height or high place
ath – new
àth – ford
baile – farm, settlement (bal, bally)
bán – white
béal – estuary
bile – tree, meeting place
bóther – road
buidhe – yellow
bun – bottom
caiseal – ringfort
caisléan – castle (cashel)
caol – strait, narrow
carraig, carreg – rock, crag
cill – church or monastery
cloch, clochàn – stone, rocky ruin (cluain)
cluain – pasture
cnoc (knock) – rounded hill, mountain
corr – rounded hill
crois – cross
currach – bog, marsh
cong – isthmus
daingean – stronghold
dearg – red
díseart – hermitage
doire – grove, oakwood
domnach – an early church (donagh)
droichead – bridge
droim – ridge, mountain crest

dubh – black, dark
eanach – marsh
èar – east
eas – waterfall
fearn – alder tree
glas – grey, green, blue (or a mix)
gleann – glen
gort – field
inis, inish – island (inch) (innis)
íochtar – lower
lag – hollow
liag – stone
lios – fortified enclosure
loch, lough – lake
machaire – plain (magh)
mhór – big (mor) big
muillean – mill
nug – new
poll – cove, pool, hollow
ráth – circular fort
ribhach – grey or mottled
rinn – promontory
ruadh – red
sliabh – mountain (slieve)
slige, sligeach – shelly (sligo)
spidéal – hospital, place of hospitality (spital)
teampall – temple
tobar – spring, well
trá(igh) – beach, shore
tulach – hill
uisce, uisge – water

IRISH TIMELINE

379-405	Niall of the Nine Hostages, King at Tara, father of the Province of Ulster Ui Neill dynasty.
400-800	Dalriada, the kingdom of counties Antrim, Ireland and Argyll, Scotland thrives.
432	St. Patrick arrives in Ireland.
500	Europeans study at Irish monasteries.
554	Columba, the monk, established a monastery at Kells.
549	Yellow Plague.
600	The end of the Old Ulliad, Kingdom of E. Ulster.
664	Yellow plague.
700	Armagh under Ui Neill control.
795	Viking raids on Scotland and Ireland.
841	Dublin founded by Vikings.
850	Irish Kings fight for dominance, Viking and Danes.
902	Dublin Vikings defeated.
950	Vikings settle on River Lee in Cork.
1000	Brain Boru, King of Munster and half of Ireland.
1014	Brian Boru fights the Ostmen and English mercenaries. He dies.
1050	O'Connors, last high kings of Ireland.
1066	Battle of Hastings - England.
1100	A century of Anglo-Norman war, foreign invasion, and church reform.
1101	Synod of Cashel: taxes, celibacy, marriage laws.
1102	Priests forbidden to marry in England.
1127	Cormac's Chapel, Cashel begun.
1152	Irish Church divided into four archbishoprics, Armagh (head), Dublin, Cashel, Tuam. New laws regarding marriage.
1154	Henry II King of England.
1169	Anglo-Norman mercenaries recruited by Diarmit MacMurchada, King of Leinster, Anglo-Norman invasion begins.
1170	Strongbow, Richard Fitzgilbert de Clare, Earl of Pembroke captures Waterford and Dublin.
1171	Irish Kings and Normans submit to Henry II of England.
1172	Christ Church Cathedral in Dublin founded.

1173	King Henry II defeats Baronial rebellion.
1177	John deCourcy invades and occupies Eastern Ulster. He builds ten forts, three castles, and six abbeys/monasteries.
1183	Rory O'Connor, last King of Ireland abdicates.
1185	Prince John arrives in Waterford as Lord of Ireland with Gerald deBarry. They take over the Suir Valley and antagonize the locals.
1205	Hugh de Lacy takes over for deCourcy.
1208-1213	England under Papal interdict.
1216	Prince Louis of France invades England.
1243	Ulster becomes a possession of England. Edward, son of Henry III, is appointed Lord of Ireland.
1258	Baronial rebellion against Henry III.
1284	Stone walls built around Cork City.
1295	Irish army sent to support King Edward against the Scots.
1296	Scottish wars for Independence.
1297	Englishmen forbidden to dress as Irishmen.
1298	Wallace defeats English at Falkirk in Scotland.
1300s	English colonizing of Ireland peaks this century.
1306	Robert the Bruce crowned King of Scotland.
1315	English defeat Edward Bruce's invasion of Ireland.
1327	Edward II deposed and murdered. Edward III.
1342	Edward III rules that all Irish, even of French or English descent, must be dismissed from all posts, and offices to be filled with English-born only.
1348-1350	Black death.
1366	Statutes of Kilkenny are written forbidding Irish-Norman marriage.
1368	Absentee landlords ordered to return to defend their lands.
1371	Robert the II, First Stuart King of Scotland, Richard the II.
1387	Earls of Ormond and Desmond warring.
1394	Richard II comes to Ireland with thirty-four thousand man army until seventy-five Irish chiefs submit. (But he is harassed in the Wicklow Mountains and flees without his army.)
1399	Henry IV - Lord Lieutenant of Ireland.
1446	Earls of Desmond and Ormond at war. Earls of Kildare rule.
1450	Richard Plantegenet, Duke of York becomes Lieutenant of Ireland.

1453	War of Roses, Kildare and Desmond side with Lancaster, Ormond with York. Yorkists win at battle of Towton.
1483	Earl of Desmond becomes Irish, "gone native" and Kildare is the only powerful noble to support the crown. The English murder Desmond's father in England and he is implored to dress and act English.
1483-85	Richard the III.
1485-1508	Henry the VII (Tudor.)
1494	Poynings Law places Irish Parliament under English authority.
1503	James IV of Scotland and Margaret Tudor marry.
1509-1533	Henry VIII. He marries Catharine of Aragon.
1541	Henry VIII made King of Ireland.
1556	Plantation of Kings and Queens County (Laois and Offaly.)
1558-1603	Queen Elizabeth's reign.
1559	Protestantism restored. Mary Queen of Scots flees.
1569-1579	Fitzmaurice revolt, much fighting, the O'Neills, and Desmond rebellions in Munster.
1570	Pope excommunicates Elizabeth.
1573	Attempted Plantation of Ulster.
1586	Plantation of Munster begins. English take one million acres, bring eighty six families.
1587	Mary Queen of Scots is executed.
1588	Spanish Armada wrecked off Ireland.
1592	Trinity College established. Elizabeth I.
1595	Rebellion of Hugh O'Neill, Earl of Tyrone.
1601	English defeat Irish and Spanish forces at Kinsale.
1603	James VI King of England and Scotland.
1607	Flight of the Earls to Europe, seeking aid against England ends Gaelic Ireland.
1609	Plantation of Ulster increases.
1613	Walls of Derry built.
1618	Forty thousand Scots in Ulster, Irish on reservations.
1627	England at war with France.
1628	Oliver Cromwell enters parliament, which will not meet again until 1644.
1641	Rebellion in Ireland. Chaos. Ulster and Munster. Massacre of Protestants.
1641	Execution of Charles I.

1642	English Civil War.
1642	Confederation of Kilkenny, a Catholic assembly.
1649	Sieges of Drogheda and Wexford by Cromwell's forces. Much butchery. They kill a third of the Irish population. Roman Catholic worship is forbidden. Catholics flee or are sent to the West Indies.
1652	Act of Settlement pays English soldiers with Irish land.
1654	Cromwellian Plantation.
1658	Cromwell dies.
1662	Charles II marries Catharine of Braganza.
1673	Test Act excludes Catholics from office. Catholics are banished, schools closed, eleven million acres seized, Catholics sent west of the Shannon River to the poorest lands.
1678	Popish plot alleged in England created hysteria.
1688	Glorious revolution of William and Mary.
1688	Seige of Derry against the Catholic Earls of Antrim. Ten thousand people die.
1689	Seige of Derry one hundred five days. James II lands with Catholic support (Jacobites,) fifteen thousand people starve behind the walls
1690	Battle of the Boyne. Thirty thousand Catholics (the Jacobites) for James II fight against thirty-six thousand Protestants for William of Orange.
1691	Treaty of Limerick, defeat of Jacobites (Catholics.) "Wild Geese" exodus to Europe.
1692	Glencoe massacre in Scotland of MacDonalds by Campbells.
1695	Laws against Catholics and dissenters enacted.
1699	English laws against Irish woolen trade enacted.
1704	Test Act bars Catholics from holding office.
1707	England and Scotland joined in Act of Union.
1719	Castletown House in County Kildare begun.
1720	Westminster gains power to legislate for Ireland.
1726	Jonathon Swift publishes *Gulliver's Travels.*
1729	Parliament House in Dublin begun.
1731	Royal Dublin Society begun.
1745	Jacobite rebellion in England.
1746	Battles of Falkirk, Scotland. Charles Stuart flees to France, tartans and arms banned in Scotland.
1756	Grand Canal construction begins from Dublin to Shannon and Barrow.

1760	George III.
1760	French land at Carrickfergus.
1762	Britain declares war on Spain.
1765	Stamp Act passes taxing American colonies.
1775-1783	Revolutionary War in America.
1776	Troops sent to America from Ireland to fight in the Revolutionary War.
1778	Catholic Relief Act passed.
1780	Home Rule demanded in Ireland.
1782	Grattan's parliament establishes legislative independence.
1782-1881	Highland land clearances in Scotland.
1789	French Revolution.
1791	United Irishmen organization founded in Belfast to change laws.
1795	Orange Order founded in County Armagh.
1796	French Invasion fleet wrecked by weather in Bantry Bay.
1798	United Irishmen rebellion in Counties Wexford and Mayo bring stricter controls and much bitterness.
1799	Combination Act enacted to unite English and Irish parliaments, although Catholics must be a minority.
1800	Act of Union imposes direct rule from London for the next one hundred years. Ireland becomes part of Britain.
1811	George III's insanity.
1803	Robert Emmet rebellion in Dublin. *Emma, Ivanhoe* written.
1823	Catholic Association established by Daniel O'Connell. National schools are established.
1828	Daniel O'Connell is elected Westminster MP (Member of Parliament.)
1829	Catholic Emancipation Act. Catholics allowed to take seats in parliament.
1832	Cholera epidemic in England.
1840	Queen Victoria marries Prince Albert.
1845-1856	Potato blight. Great Famine begins, the worst year is 1847. Many emigrate. Queen's Colleges established in Belfast, Cork, and Galway.
1848	Young Ireland's Rebellion rejects Daniel O'Connell's non-violent politics.
1850	Irish Republican Brotherhood (IRB) funded by Irish Americans. to bring about an Irish Republic.

1867	Fenian Rebellion attempts to gain Irish Independence by force, bombings.
1871	Trade Unions were established in England.
1873	Home Rule League founded.
1874	Ernest Shackleton born in Kilkeen.
1877	C.S. Parnell turns "Home Rulers" into a viable political party.
1880	Parnell leads Irish Parliamentary Party.
1882	Assassination of Lord Cavandish in Phoenix Park.
1884	GAA (Gaelic Athletic Association) founded.
1886	First Home Rule Bill is defeated.
1893	Gaelic League founded.
1897	*Dracula* - Bram Stoker, and The *Gadfly* by Ethel Voynich written.
1890	Parnell ousted from Home Rule movement. Parnell scandal.
1903	Land Act established to allow tenants to purchase land with government aid.
1904	Abbey Theater opens.
1905	Sinn Féin founded: the Irish are free and no laws should be made without their consent.
1905	Ulster Unionist Council formed. Irish Industrial association. Ancient Order of Hibernians is reorganized.
1909	Volta Theater in Dublin opens with James Joyce as manager.
1911	Titanic launched in Belfast.
1913	Ulster Volunteer Force, Irish Volunteers and Irish Citizens Army.
1913	Lockout strike in Dublin.
1914	England declares war on Germany.
1914	Home Rule bill passed, but not implemented. James Joyce's *Dubliners* published. Lusitania sinks off Cork coast.
1916	"Easter Rising" in Dublin, Irish Republic proclaimed. Sixteen leaders executed.
1919	First Dáil sits in Dublin following Westminster elections.
1919-1921	War of Independence for Ireland against England.
1919	IRA formed. Many atrocities on both sides.
1920	Government of Ireland Act partitions Ireland.
1921	Truce. Anglo-Irish Agreement.
1922	Irish Free State established. They enact constitution.
1922	Michael Collins killed in ambush. James Joyce's, *Ulysses*, published in Paris.

1922-1923 Civil war in Irish Free State.

1923   W.B. Yeats receives Nobel Prize for Literature.

1926   G. B. Shaw receives Nobel Prize for Literature.

1928   Women in England allowed to vote.

1932-1939 Economic war with Britain.

1937   New Constitution for Ireland/Eire.

1939-1945 England declares war on Germany. Ireland declares neutrality although ten thousand Irish serve with England.

1948   Irish Republic declared.

1949   **Irish Republic is born.**

1956-1962 Bombings and protest in Northern Ireland.

1964-1969 Civil rights protests lead to Northern Ireland Civil Rights Association.

1969   British troops arrive in Northern Ireland. Samuel Beckett receives Nobel Prize in Literature.

1971   British Embassy burned in Dublin. Internment without trial in Northern Ireland.

1972   Bloody Sunday. Thirteen in Derry die. Stormont parliament is suspended. Direct rule from London.

1973   Republic of Ireland joins EEC (European Economic Community (E.U.)
           Sean MacBride, a founder of Amnesty International and human rights campaigner, wins Nobel Peace Prize.

1974   Ulster workers strike in Northern Ireland.

1976   British Ambassador assassinated in Dublin.

1977   Mairead Corrigan and Betty Williams receive Nobel Peace Prize.

1979   Earl Mountbattan assassinated in Sligo.

1981   Republican hunger strike in Northern Ireland, ten die, including Bobby Sands, elected MP.

1985   Anglo-Irish Agreement between governments.

1987   Enniskillen Remembrance Day bombing. Eleven die.

1991   Mary Robinson 1st woman president of the Republic.

1993   Downing Street Declaration: Right of people of Ireland to self-rule and solve issues between the Republic and Northern Ireland by majority.

1994   Irish Republican Army (IRA) and Combined Loyalist Military Command agree on ceasefire.

1996	Seamus Heaney awarded Nobel Prize in Literature. IRA ceasefire ends. Canary Wharf bombing by IRA.
1997	Resume ceasefire.
1998	Belfast Good Friday Agreement for Peace. David Trimble and John Hume awarded Nobel Peace Prize.
1999	Northern Ireland Assembly operating as regional parliament. National Museum opens in Dublin.
2000	Millenium Forest project to plant a tree for each member of the Republic was formed.
2002	Republic of Ireland currency becomes Euro. Northern Ireland Assembly suspended by Britain.
2003	Democratic Unionist Party (DUP) and Sinn Féin are the dominant political parties.
2004	Northern Ireland Assembly remains suspended.
2005	The IRA agrees to disarm voluntarily.
2006	Twenty year strategy launched to create bilingual Irish-English society.
2008	Global financial crisis sinks economy.
2010	Austerity program, EU bailout.
2013	Recession, Republic exits bailout program having fulfilled conditions.

Counties
of Ireland

DONEGAL

LONDONDERRY ANTRIM

BELFAST

TYRONE

DONEGAL

FERMANAGH

DOWN

ARMAGH

MONAGHAN

SLIGO

LEITRIM

CAVAN

LOUTH

ROSCOMMON

DROGHEDA

MAYO

LONGFORD

WEST MEATH

MEATH

GALWAY

DUBLIN
DUBLIN

GALWAY

OFFALY

KILDARE

WICKLOW

LAOIS

CLARE

TIPPERARY

KILKENNY

CARLOW

WEXFORD

LIMERICK

WEXFORD

LIMERICK

TIPPERARY

WATERFORD

KERRY

CORK

CORK

About the Author

LESLIE LEE is an author, artist, and poet. She has a way of making things happen with adventure and creativity as hallmarks of her life. She built her own tiny cabin in 1977 where she began the book about her grandfather, *Backcountry Ranger in Glacier National Park, 1910 to 1913: The Diaries and Photographs of Norton Pearl* published in 1994. Lee gave the Chicago-based company, U.S. Robotics, Inc. a good start in the 1980s, raised her three children in northern Michigan, and worked ten years building Pine Hollow Country House to become a charitable institute.

An active philanthropist and dedicated environmentalist, Lee co-founded Archangel Ancient Tree Archive in 2008 where she sponsored the major collection of clones from some of the oldest Coast Redwoods, Giant Sequoias, Black Willows, and Irish Oaks. In 2014 Lee wrote the book *Sacred Space: Pine Hollow*. Lee lives in northern Michigan where she is compiling thirty years of travel art and writing into books including paintings, charts, maps, and poetry.

"What a delight to be 'found' by three sisters and their cousin in 2007 and to discover that they too were our cousins!!! It was thrilling to sit down and look through the evidence and realize that we shared common ancestry from the turn of the 19th century. Such an enthusiasm for ancestors and such warmth to connect with newly found cousins. We enjoyed meeting Leslie, Liz, Jenni, and Josie and to feel a connection which echoed across the decades, even centuries. It has been a joy to get to know them, to visit them in Michigan and to sense the common roots. This book brings it all together - a skillful blending of the story of sisters, of their search for their Irish ancestors and the subtlety, while telling this intensely personal story, to tell also the complex story of Ireland. Leslie has blended the chapters together with sensitivity capping many with a fitting quote from her poetry collection, *Sacred Space*. This is a great story and a good guide to any who may similarly seek to find out more of their family history."

—GEORGE AND VIVIENNE NIXON

CPSIA information can be obtained
at www.ICGtesting.com
Printed in the USA
BVHW021402230619
551697BV00001B/1/P

9 780099 150224